CLASSIC MOVIES

CLASSIC MOVIES

NEIL SINYARD

CHANCELLOR
PRESS

CONTENTS

This book is for Lesley

FRONT ENDPAPERS: A rehearsal scene from *42nd Street*. Far left, by the proscenium arch, is Dick Powell. Centre, his back to the camera, is the producer, Warner Baxter. His assistant, George E. Stone, is on stage, also back to camera. To his right is the star, Bebe Daniels.

TITLE PAGE, left: Toshiro Mifune as the bandit and Machiko Kyo as the nobleman's wife in *Rashomon*.
Right: *Camille*. Armand returns to Marguerite, only to find her dying. Greta Garbo and Robert Taylor.

BACK ENDPAPERS: The onset of Revolution in *Dr Zhivago*. The soldiers of the Russian army turn on their officers.

This edition published in 1993 by
Chancellor Press
part of Reed Consumer Books Limited
Michelin House, 81 Fulham Road,
London SW3 6RB
and Auckland, Melbourne, Singapore and Toronto

Copyright © 1985, 1993 Reed International Books Limited

ISBN 1 8515 23774

A catalogue record for this book is available from
the British Library

Produced by Mandarin Offset
Printed and bound in Malaysia

SILENTS

Intolerance (1926) · *The Cabinet of Dr Caligari* (1919)
Greed (1923) · *Battleship Potemkin* (1925) · *The General* (1926)

Spectacle and comedy were two of the main features of the silent cinema,
revealing the potential of the new medium to excited audiences.
LEFT: The grand manner in Griffith's *Intolerance*. The approaches to the
temple, before the Fall of Babylon.
ABOVE: *The General*. Buster Keaton rescues his girl, played by Marian Mack.

INTOLERANCE

USA 1916

DIRECTED BY
D. W. GRIFFITH

Photography: *G. W. 'Billy' Bitzer*
Wark Producing Corporation.
183 mins

Leading players:
*Lillian Gish, Mae Marsh,
Robert Harron, Miriam Cooper,
Walter Long.*

In the movies' age of innocence no one dreamt bigger than D. W. Griffifth. After learning his craft on hundreds of shorts at Biograph Studios, and after the colossal success of his film about the American Civil War and the Reconstruction period, *The Birth of a Nation* (1915), Griffith now embarked on his most monumental venture, *Intolerance*. The film's nobility of theme and massive formal conception were designed to break all previously-known boundaries of the cinema.

The opening title declares the basic theme: 'how hatred and intolerance, through all the ages, have battled against love and charity'. The film tells four stories which exemplify different facets of intolerance through the ages: a contemporary story of heartless employers, exploited workers and moral crusaders; the massacre of the Huguenots in 1572 on St Bartholomew's Day; the fall of Babylon to the Persians because of the treachery of the priests; and the Crucifixion.

In crosscutting the four stories, Griffith had a precise design in his head. 'The stories will begin like four currents looked at from a hilltop,' he said. 'But as they flow, they grow nearer and nearer together, and faster and faster, until in the end, in the last act, they mingle in one mighty river of expressed emotion.' The realism of the modern story contrasts with the staggering spectacle of the Babylon section, and the excitement of the final chase to save the pardoned hero from execution in the modern story is crosscut with the measured procession to Calvary. The stories are linked by what Griffith called 'a golden thread – a fairy girl with sunlit hair – her hand on the cradle of humanity – eternally rocking'.

Griffith's first version of *Intolerance* ran for eight hours. Even in its slimmer version, the public at the time seemed bewildered by separate narratives which interrupted rather than linked with each other, and were perhaps unsympathetic to its pacifist message when the country was readying itself for war. Nevertheless, the film's vivid sense of movement, its narrative boldness, its experimentation with shape and size, its stunning use of close-up detail (like the famous shot of the clenched hand to suggest tension during a dramatic moment in a trial) had a far-reaching impact on film aesthetics. Its method anticipates the social realism and human psychology of Stroheim and Vidor, the montage miracles of Eisenstein, and the epic grandeur of Abel Gance.

Intolerance remains a milestone. The seriousness of its theme conferred a new respectability on what had seemed to many to be a low and callow art form. Its grandiose conception showed the cinema as a technological form nevertheless capable of being moulded by the genius of one man. And Griffith's conception of cinema had an idealism that one can feel pulsing through *Intolerance* and makes the film even now an awesome experience. 'With the universal language of motion pictures,' he said, 'the true meaning of the brotherhood of man will have been established throughout the earth.'

The chief innovation of *Intolerance* was its interweaving of four different stories, set at different times of history.
LEFT: In the modern story, Robert Harron is on the scaffold, about to be hanged, before his last-minute pardon.
BELOW: Mae Marsh listens intently in the courtroom for the verdict on her husband, who is being tried for murder. The shot is a good example of Griffith's dramatic use of close-up.
BOTTOM LEFT: The massacre of the Huguenots on St Bartholomew's Day, Griffith's example of the extremes of religious intolerance.
RIGHT: A war chariot, a detail from Griffith's spectacular reconstruction of the Fall of Babylon.
BOTTOM RIGHT: Christ carries the cross on the road to Calvary. Griffith daringly crosscuts his re-creation of the Crucifixion with the race against time in the modern story to save the hero from hanging.

RIGHT: The twisted world of *The Cabinet of Dr Caligari* has haunted film-makers for decades, influencing their visual presentation of terror and psychological disorder. Caligari (Werner Krauss) watches disdainfully as the story-teller, Francis (Friedrich Feher) and the doctor (Rudolf Lettinger) examine the somnambulist Cesare (Conrad Veidt).

BELOW: Cesare carries off the girl (Lil Dagover) after the murder of the hero's friend. Notice the deliberately unreal, stylized décor to reflect a world out of joint.

BELOW RIGHT: Francis, the hero, searches for the secret of Caligari's cabinet. 'I will not rest,' he says, 'until I have fully fathomed the terrible things that are happening around me.'

FAR RIGHT: The bleak asylum garden in which Francis narrates his terrifying tale. The final shock is yet to come – that the director of the asylum is none other than Caligari himself.

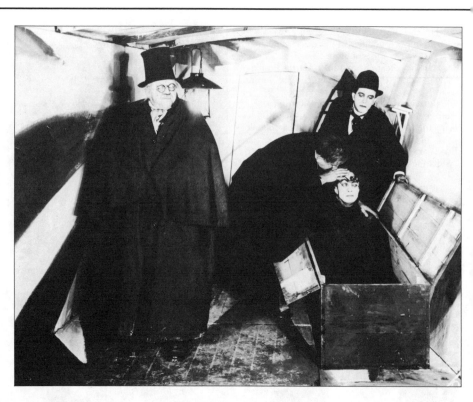

The Cabinet of Dr Caligari

Germany 1919
Directed by Robert Wiene

Producer: *Rudolf Meinert*
Screenplay: *Carl Mayer and Hans Janowitz*
Photography: *Willy Hameister*
Design: *Walter Reimann, Herman Warm, Walter Rohrig*
Decla Bioscop. 81 mins

Leading players:
Werner Krauss, Conrad Veidt, Lil Dagover, Friedrich Feher.

When the producer received the script of *The Cabinet of Dr Caligari*, he passed it to the designers who realized that such a strange creation would require extraordinary sets. The style they fixed on was Expressionism, one designed to evoke and express extreme mental states by distorting the details of the external physical world.

The plot concerns a series of murders which are traceable to a fairground entertainer, Dr Caligari (Werner Krauss) and his sinister assistant, the somnambulist Cesare (Conrad Veidt). The twist in the tale is the revelation that the story is being related by a lunatic in an asylum, suffering under the delusion that the director of the institution is none other than Caligari himself. This final twist throws doubt on whether the story is real or fantasy, and whether the tale is the symptom of the narrator's madness or the cause of it.

This story within a story structure was director Robert Wiene's idea, and displeased the writers. After the tragedy and waste of World War I their script was conceived as a protest against mad authority, particularly symbolized in the oppressive relationship between the evil Caligari and his helpless servant, Cesare. By revealing the story to be the ravings of a madman, the film, they thought, tamed their angrily anti-authoritarian theme.

However, the ending of the film might not be as compromised as they feel, and indeed might take the menace a step further. The film's visual world remains twisted and tortured, reflecting a world of continuing ambiguity and paranoia in which nobody is to be trusted. Also, given the menacing appearance of Werner Krauss, the revelation that he is the director of the institution in which the narrator is imprisoned – in other words, another authority figure who can tranquillize people to act according to his will – is hardly reassuring. Might not the hypnotic power of the authority figure, coupled with the apprehension that that authority itself is evil and corrupt, be seen as a sinister foreshadowing of Fascism? In his study of post-war German cinema, the critic Siegfried Kracauer had no doubts on that score: *From Caligari to Hitler*, he called it.

For some cinéastes, it is something of an abomination, a décor film more than a director's film, whose artificiality is a denial of the film camera's unique capacity to photograph the real world. Eisenstein called it 'a barbaric carnival', whilst writers like Ezra Pound and George Orwell dismissed it as a static exercise in morbid psychology. But Virginia Woolf admired its capacity for visualizing inner emotions, its ability, as she saw it, to show the '*shape* of fear'. René Clair thought it affirmed that the 'only interesting truth is the subjective'. Its blend of Freud and the fairground has had an enormous influence on directors like Alfred Hitchcock, Orson Welles and Fritz Lang (who was originally invited to direct). In nearly every film noir, horror film or the avant-garde, one can sense the ghost of Caligari conjuring Cesare out of his box to roam free in the nocturnal world of the subconscious.

GREED

USA 1923

DIRECTED BY
ERICH VON STROHEIM

Screenplay: *Erich von Stroheim*.
Based on the novel, *McTeague*
by Frank Norris.
Titles by *June Mathis*
Photography: *William Daniels,
Ben Reynolds*
MGM. 104 mins

Leading players:
*Gibson Gowland, Zasu Pitts,
Jean Hersholt*.

Contrary to legend, Erich von Stroheim was not descended from Prussian nobility but was the son of a Jewish tradesman who had settled in Vienna. Nevertheless, every aspect of Stroheim's career seemed designed to perpetuate the image of aristocratic grandeur. Having served as an assistant on *Intolerance* it is also possible that he had absorbed some of Griffith's megalomania. All of that extravagance was to pour into his film of Frank Norris's novel, *McTeague*. *Greed* is one of the legends of the cinema, as is, unfortunately, the tragedy behind its making.

McTeague is a dentist, whose relationship with his friend Marcus is strained when he becomes engaged to Marcus's former girl friend, Trina. The event which

TOP LEFT: The wedding of McTeague (Gibson Gowland) and Trina (Zasu Pitts).
CENTRE: Trina (left) counts her money, which will soon become an obsession and destroy her marriage to McTeague (right).
BOTTOM LEFT: The disintegration of the marriage leads to violence and murder. The drunken McTeague attacks his wife.
TOP RIGHT: The deadly emotions of the characters lead to Death Valley, where McTeague escapes after murdering Trina.
BOTTOM RIGHT: The final confrontation between McTeague and Marcus (Jean Hersholt), who has followed McTeague to Death Valley out of a lust for gold and revenge. The theme of greed and the desert setting were to be a clear influence on John Huston's famous film, *The Treasure of the Sierra Madre* (1948). John Grierson called Stroheim 'the director of all directors', largely because of Stroheim's perfectionism and his disregard of his backers. Even in its mutilated form *Greed* is a milestone of film realism.

changes them all is Trina's winning of 5,000 dollars in a lottery. After the marriage, she becomes a neurotic miser; McTeague a drunken and sadistic brute, who will murder his wife for money; and Marcus an envious fop who will betray McTeague. The two former friends are to meet finally in a murderous confrontation in Death Valley.

Apparently, Stroheim had first read the novel when an impoverished dishwasher in New York, and resolved to film it with absolute fidelity, shooting as far as possible on the novel's locations in San Francisco, commandeering blocks of houses and tearing down walls to facilitate the filming of interiors. The Death Valley sequences were filmed on the spot, which almost killed some of the cast and crew. To emphasize the novel's theme of people's corruption by money, he experimented with colour by having gold painted in on some prints of the film for certain details – candle flames, brass knobs on the bedsteads, the birdcage found in the desert.

Most outrageously, Stroheim insisted on filming the whole novel, page by page. The result was a finished work that ran for forty-two reels (without a break, roughly seven hours) which Stroheim himself cut down to twenty-four. However, the Goldwyn Company, with which Stroheim had started the film, had merged with Metro in the interim to become MGM. The new regime, under Louis B. Mayer and Irving Thalberg (who made the famous crack about Stroheim's being a 'footage fetishist') decreed that it should be cut to ten, reducing the film, in Stroheim's view, to a 'mutilated child'.

Even in its diminished form, it is remarkable. 'I wish to show real life,' said Stroheim, 'with its degradation, baseness, violence, sensuality and, a singular contrast in the midst of this filth, purity.' Such stark contrasts inform the most memorable images: a kiss next to a sewer; a wedding reception, in which a funeral procession is simultaneously visible through a window; a murder, ironically framed by Christmas tinsel. The remarkable conclusion shows McTeague handcuffed to a corpse in Death Valley, his money also a dead weight, and with a masterly succession of distanced shots reducing him to a speck of dust in the wilderness. 'You were ten years ahead of your time,' Billy Wilder told Stroheim. With that imperious manner which he never lost, Stroheim replied: 'No – twenty.'

ABOVE: Sailors on the *Potemkin* inspect the rotten meat, crawling with maggots. ABOVE LEFT: The men who have refused to eat the food are lined up to be shot, but the firing squad refuses to obey orders. TOP RIGHT: The mutiny on the *Potemkin*. CENTRE: Crowds gather on the Odessa steps to cheer the mutineers. BOTTOM RIGHT: The massacre on the Odessa steps. The Cossacks advance like a machine over the dead bodies. FAR RIGHT: Eisenstein intercuts general shots of carnage with more specific close-up detail to emphasize the horror of the attack. In a famous detail, a woman carries the body of a dead child up the steps, a striking figure of mute reproach. Sergei Eisenstein always said that the Russian Revolution made an artist out of him, giving him the freedom to pursue his own choice of career. *Battleship Potemkin* is unquestionably his most memorable revolutionary film.

BATTLESHIP POTEMKIN

USSR 1925

DIRECTED BY SERGEI M. EISTENSTEIN

Screenplay: *Sergei M. Eisenstein, Nina Agadzhanova-Shutko*
Photography: *Eduard Tisse, V. Popov*
72 mins

Leading players:
Alexander Antonov, Vladimar Barsky, Repnikova

Battleship Potemkin is a revolutionary film on a revolutionary subject. The original intention was to make a film that would celebrate the twentieth anniversary of the 1905 Revolution by showing several key events of that year. But it was ultimately decided to concentrate on one particular event: the mutiny of the sailors on the *Potemkin*. This incident seemed to contain all the main issues of the original struggle and showed the routing of injustice and oppression by brotherhood and collective action.

If the film has the burning immediacy of an on-the-spot news report, this is attributable to the circumstances in which the film was made. Because it obviously had to be ready by the end of the year, the film was conceived and executed with lightning rapidity. It was shot in a week and edited in a fortnight, its final reel being delivered to the cinema actually during the first performance. Shooting had begun in Leningrad but, because of adverse weather conditions, had to be moved to Odessa, and Eisenstein turned whatever conditions he found to remarkable advantage. The scene where a sailor is buried was shot in misty conditions because they did not have time to wait for the weather to change; it makes for an appropriately melancholy, wistful effect. The film's most famous scene – the massacre on the Odessa steps, when the Cossack army advances on the crowd – was an inspiration of Eisenstein's, when he first saw the setting and decided he must use it. Historically dubious, perhaps, but cinematically a sensation.

In this scene, Eisenstein brought into play his theories about film practice, particularly his ideas about montage (the meaning produced when separate shots are grouped together in a particular order). The Odessa steps sequence is so astonishing because it reproduces a sense of chaos and carnage through rigid selection and organization. The conflict in the scene is intensified through the calculated conflict of the images: still shots followed by moving shots, upward movement by downward movement, marching boots by fleeing people, individual detail by mass panic, all controlled within a carefully regulated tempo and rhythm. The logic of space and time is suddenly distorted to convey the horror of the event. A student's face conveys individual helplessness at mass horror; a Cossack with a slashing sabre exemplifies the brutality of the massacre; the unforgettable close-up of an old woman's face, her glasses broken and blood streaming from her eye, is an image which proclaims the film's rage at the soldiers' action.

Eisenstein was only in his mid-twenties when he made *Potemkin* and the film is infused with a youthful polemical passion as well as a young technician's delight in the tools of his craft. It demonstrates the cinema's capacity for political persuasion, raising propaganda to the level of art.

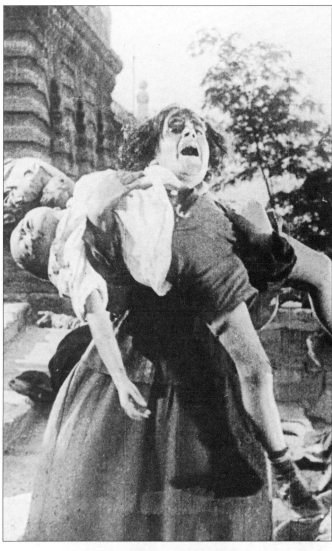

THE GENERAL

USA 1926
DIRECTED BY
BUSTER KEATON AND
CLYDE BRUCKMAN

Screenplay: *Buster Keaton,*
Clyde Bruckman
Adaptation by *Al Boasberg,*
Charles Smith
Photography: *Dev Jennings,*
Bert Haines
United Artists. 82 minutes

Leading players:
Buster Keaton, Marian Mack.

Buster Keaton was a natural, which might be the reason that this film was underrated for so long. 'By no means as good as Mr Keaton's previous efforts', 'long and slow', and 'a pretty trite and stodgy piece of screen craft', were some of the contemporary views of *The General*. Nowadays, the graceful athleticism and technical precision that Keaton displays so nonchalantly in the film look not simply inventive but unique.

Like the locomotive that Buster chases during the film, the plot of *The General*, whilst having its diversions, proceeds mainly on a straight line. Keaton plays an engineer at the time of the American Civil

War who has two loves – his engine and his girl. When both are stolen by Northern spies, he chases the engine by hand-cart, penny-farthing and on foot, eventually rescuing the girl behind enemy lines. He then turns the engine and the plot into reverse, heading back to the South past the same landmarks as before and with brilliant variations on earlier jokes.

It is a classic Keaton situation: the challenge and the chase, with the ultimate effect of redeeming himself in the eyes of his girl who has spurned him when he has been rejected as a soldier. As often in his films, man has to attain mastery over the machine. The situations call for that slow-burning but indomitable Keaton ingenuity, whereby a problem is scrutinized then deftly solved, whether it be the removal of an obstacle on the track, or stealing a kiss from his girl whilst simultaneously saluting the passing soldiers, or contriving the exit from a room of two small boys who are spoiling his courting. Every emotion is made eloquent by that inimitable face, a map of concentration, stoicism and nuance that made Keaton one of the subtlest of screen actors.

Technically, the film is staggering. The filming of the locomotives has smoothness, variety and excitement, and the battle-scenes have the authenticity of Civil War photographs. The visual effects range from a hilarious iris shot, as Keaton spies through a cigarette burn in a tablecloth, to an awe-inspiring image of the Northern train as it falls through the Rock River

bridge into the water (reputed to be the most expensive single take of the silent cinema).

Keaton described *The General* as 'a page out of history'. He was always concerned to make his films look as real as possible, which meant doing the stunts himself and mastering a visual style that was a model of unpretentious fluency and economy. In *The General*, the realism results in a film where the romance, the suspense and the conflict seem as genuine as the comedy. Whilst constructing some of his most audacious slapstick routines, Keaton – with his left hand, as it were – was also making the best film ever about the American Civil War.

FAR LEFT: Johnny Gray (Buster Keaton), with his two young followers, inspects his beloved engine, 'The General'.
BOTTOM LEFT: Johnny is spurned by his girl, Annabelle (Marian Mack), who is dismayed by his failure to join the Southern Army. 'If you lose this war,' Johnny has said, 'don't blame me.'
CENTRE: Johnny's girl has been captured and he has pursued her behind enemy lines. Here, as the Northern soldiers debate strategy, he hides under the table, planning his next move.
BELOW: In the film's most spectacular effect, the Northern train plunges through the bridge into the river. Keaton can be seen here, surveying the wreckage.
BOTTOM: Johnny rescues his girl and turns the engine and the plot into reverse, heading for home. Since his death in 1966, Buster Keaton's reputation has soared, and *The General* was Keaton's own favourite. It is now generally regarded as his best film and the greatest of all silent comedies.

WESTERNS

Stagecoach (1939) · *High Noon* (1952) · *Shane* (1953) ·
Rio Bravo (1959) · *The Wild Bunch* (1969)

Of all the film forms, the Western is the one which particularly displays the cinema's gift for utilizing breathtaking locations and staging exciting action.
LEFT: The most famous of all Western settings, Monument Valley, across which the cavalry is escorting the stage in *Stagecoach*.
ABOVE: One of the great Western heroes, Gary Cooper, in his most famous role, the marshal in *High Noon* who faces the four outlaws alone.

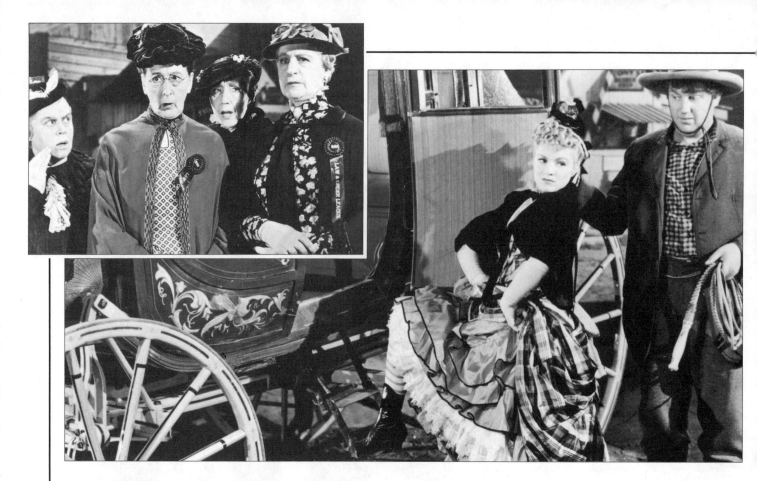

STAGECOACH

USA 1939
DIRECTED BY JOHN FORD

Executive producer:
Walter Wanger
Screenplay: *Dudley Nichols*
Based on the story
Stage to Lordsburg
by Ernest Haycox
Music: *Richard Hageman,*
W. Franke Harling, John Leipold,
Leo Shuken, Louis Gruenberg
Photography: *Bert Glennon*
United Artists. 97 mins

Leading players:
John Wayne, Claire Trevor,
Thomas Mitchell, John Carradine,
Andy Devine, Donald Meek,
Louise Platt, George Bancroft,
Tim Holt, Berton Churchill.

'My name's John Ford,' he said, 'I make westerns.' Prior to Ford, the western as a film genre had scarcely been taken seriously: 'movies about horses for horses', was writer Ben Hecht's scathing description of them. In subsequent films such as *My Darling Clementine* (1945), *Fort Apache*

(1948), *The Searchers* (1956) and *The Man who shot Liberty Valance* (1962) Ford was to show that the western was about many things: the emergence of civilization from a wilderness, the gap between history and legend, and the meaning and destiny of America.

Stagecoach united Ford with a setting and a star. As a change from the studio-bound westerns of the decade, Ford shot his locations in Monument Valley, an awesome setting that seemed to expand his western dramas into epic contemplations of the relation between man and landscape. For a first starring role, Ford gave an opportunity to John Wayne in the part of the Ringo Kid, introducing the character in the film with a memorable visual flourish and providing a part of dogged indomitable heroism that Wayne was to make his trademark for the next forty years.

The plot could not be simpler. For reasons of their own, a group of social misfits travel by stage from Tonto to Lordsburg, on the way being attacked by Apaches. The action scenes are handled with dashing confidence: the chase across the salt flats between stagecoach and Indians and the last-minute rescue (literally, in answer to a prayer) by the cavalry; the final shoot-out in a darkened Lordsburg street between Ringo and the Plummer boys. Conventionally, the Indians are

the forces of chaos, but they are not the only ones. As the saloon girl Dallas (Claire Trevor) says when being thrown out of Tonto by the stuffy and righteous citizens: 'There are worse things than Apaches.' *Stagecoach* is not only about the threats from savage primitives, but about the taunts of social prejudice.

'A powerful story of strange people!' said a poster of the time, and that it is. Ringo, Dallas, and the drunkard Doc Boone (an Oscar-winning performance from Thomas Mitchell), who are all outsiders, essentially team up against the rest of the passengers – a Southern gambler, an Eastern lady, an apparently respectable banker – who treat them with disdain. Served by an expertly characterized and structured script by Dudley Nichols, Ford gives his sympathies to the social renegades, and he dismisses those representatives of respectability as either snobs or crooks. Ford was an astute observer of behaviour as well as spectacle. *Stagecoach* is a social comedy about the upper and lower orders as well as an exciting adventure. Like most great westerns, *Stagecoach* is also a shrewd study of human nature under stress. As the stage moves from the trappings of civilization into the wilderness, the characters will confront not only Apaches but themselves.

FAR LEFT: 'There are worse things than Apaches.' The Law-and-Order League insists that saloon girl Dallas leave town. Dallas (Claire Trevor) defiantly climbs on to the stage, watched by the driver (Andy Devine).

LEFT: The first appearance of the Ringo Kid (John Wayne, right), as he stops the stage and confronts the sheriff (George Bancroft, holding rifle).

BELOW: At the halt, the passengers become better acquainted. The groupings are important: the outsiders, Dallas and Ringo, are seated together; Doc Boone (Thomas Mitchell, far right) watches the gesticulating whisky salesman (Donald Meek). Standing on the right, the soldier (Tim Holt) and the gambler (John Carradine) hover protectively over the refined Mrs Mallory (Louise Platt). Seated is the banker (Berton Churchill).

BOTTOM LEFT: The stagecoach crosses the river.

RIGHT: Apaches appear at the top of a ridge, just as the stage appears to have reached safety. John Ford was the great poet of America's pioneering past and *Stagecoach* was a Western that set new standards of action and characterization.

HIGH NOON

USA 1952

DIRECTED BY
FRED ZINNEMANN

Producer: *Stanley Kramer*
Screenplay: *Carl Foreman*
Based on the story *The Tin Star*
by John W. Cunningham
Music: *Dimitri Tiomkin*
(Title song by Dimitri Tiomkin and
Ned Washington)
Photography: *Floyd Crosby*
United Artists. 85 mins

Leading players:
*Gary Cooper, Grace Kelly,
Lloyd Bridges, Katy Jurado,
Thomas Mitchell.*

*And I must face a man who hates me,
Or lie a coward, a craven coward,
Or lie a coward in my grave.*

These lyrics from the famous ballad of
High Noon define the dilemma at the
heart of the film. Three outlaws have
ridden into town and await their leader on
the noon train, at which time they plan to
avenge themselves on the marshal who
had sent them to prison. Marshal Kane
(Gary Cooper) is exhorted by the townspeople to leave, believing that, if he does,
maybe there will be no trouble. But,
although newly married and technically
retired, Kane is too proud to run. To do so,
he believes, would be a denial of what he
had achieved and the values by which he
lives.

High Noon has been described by its
detractors as 'a western for those who do
not like westerns', but such a description
tends only to highlight its originality.
Unlike the conventional western, it has a
bleached and gritty visual surface and its
main character conveys a human strain
and vulnerability that adds considerably to
the tension. (Gary Cooper's skilful performance won him an Oscar.) The suspense is intensified still further by the time
factor and with shots of clocks that loom
larger like instruments of doom as the
danger draws nearer and the possibility of
help for the marshal recedes. Unlike the
heroic showdown in *Stagecoach*, the final
shoot-out is a strategic, ignoble affair that

spreads messily across the town's deserted streets.

For director Fred Zinnemann, *High Noon* was less of a western than a study of conscience and character. Like the main protagonists of other famous Zinnemann films, *From Here to Eternity* (1953), *The Nun's Story* (1959) and *A Man For All Seasons* (1966), Marshal Kane is a man who sticks to his principles and will not bend them to suit the situation. His unwillingness to compromise forces the townspeople off the fence and compels them to confront inadequacies and weaknesses within themselves. Within its traditional format, *High Noon* asks serious questions about the cost of individual courage and about the consequences of a communal refusal to stand up to evil.

At any time, these are important issues. When the film came out, they were explosive. America was in the grip of an anti-communist witch hunt orchestrated by Senator McCarthy, and Hollywood was reeling from the investigations of the House of UnAmerican Activities Committee into the political beliefs of the community. For its writer Carl Foreman, who was shortly to be blacklisted and sent into exile, *High Noon* was a passionate study of a community corrupted by fear. The scene in the church, where the Marshal seeks help and is essentially put

on trial by townspeople fearing danger through association, must have struck many uncomfortable chords in the Hollywood of 1952. The film's most courageous gesture is saved until last, when the Marshal's opinion of the community he has served and saved is crystallized by his action of contemptuously throwing his tin star into the dust.

FAR LEFT: Just married to Amy (Grace Kelly) and preparing to leave town, the marshal (Gary Cooper) reads the wire informing him that the outlaw Frank Miller has been released from prison.
LEFT: The marshal's wife meets his former lover, Helen Ramirez (Katy Jurado). The physical difference is striking, the wife's white wedding dress (symbolizing the marshal's hope for the future) contrasting with Jurado's dark clothing (symbolizing the marshal's past). 'Why is he doing this?' the wife asks. 'If you don't know, I can't tell you,' Helen replies.
BOTTOM LEFT: The marshal seeks help in the saloon: notice how all avoid looking at him.
CENTRE: The noon train has arrived and Miller joins his three outlaw friends, intent on revenge.
BELOW: Miller (Harry Shannon) and his partner (Robert Wilke) advance on the marshal.
BOTTOM: The marshal, his challenge faced – and overcome – alone, leaves the town with his wife. The tin star, his symbol of office, lies in the dust where he has discarded it.

SHANE

USA 1953

DIRECTED BY
GEORGE STEVENS

Producer: *George Stevens*
Screenplay: *A. B. Guthrie Jr.*
Based on the novel by
Jack Schaefer.
Music: *Victor Young*
Photography: *Loyal Griggs*
Paramount. 118 mins

Leading players:
*Alan Ladd, Van Heflin,
Jean Arthur, Brandon de Wilde,
Jack Palance.*

Shane is the romantic western par excellence. The title character is a buckskin-clad gunfighter who descends into a Wyoming valley and into the middle of a range war between homesteaders and cattlemen. His guns ultimately rid the valley of evil, but his violence now has no place in the society he has saved, and he must ride out as mysteriously as he came.

Because the action is largely seen through the eyes of a child, the film glows with a golden, dream-like vision in which the characters loom larger than life. Ennobled by Victor Young's majestic main theme, Shane becomes an idealization of goodness, and Alan Ladd's performance has a gentle gravity and grace. In contrast, Jack Palance's opposing gunslinger, Wilson, is the personification of evil, a black-gloved Lucifer who deals out Death.

If the child sees the drama simply in terms of good and evil, the film offers more complicated perspectives. It shows the contamination of violence, whereby Shane is unable to live down his past. It is also a film with strong implications of repressed emotion and unrequited love. Shane's devotion to the Starrett family seems barely to conceal his growing affection for Joe Starrett's wife, Marian. For her part, Shane seems to enkindle a repressed, almost forbidden, romantic longing, a secret craving for a more exciting life. Their farewell scene, in which both step back from commitment into roles whose dissatisfaction they now openly acknowledge, is all the more romantic because of its restraint – the most passionate handshake in movies.

Beautifully acted by Van Heflin and Jean Arthur, the domestic scenes have great ease and naturalness, but the set-pieces are excitingly stylized. A bar-room brawl is a ballet of brutality. The gunfight between Wilson and a homesteader and the fight between Shane and Starrett seem to provoke Shakespearian disruptions in nature. In the first, an impending thunderstorm throws ominous shadows and cracks of doom across the confrontation. In the second, the fight's turbulence is heightened by Marian's shrill screams and the hysteria of the horses. During the struggle, they fall across the stump that Shane has earlier helped Starrett to uproot – a reminder that, once again and definitively, Shane must complete something that Starrett has started.

The showdown between Shane and Wilson has a ritualistic grandeur. And the farewell scene between Shane and little Joe (the faultless Brandon de Wilde) brings all the themes beautifully together. 'Tell your mother there need be no more guns in the valley,' says Shane, before placing his hand on the boy's head, as if annointing him for the onset of maturity. As Joey shouts after Shane, the echoing hills ('And mother wants you . . . wants you . . . I know she does . . . she does') intensify the poignancy of his cries and multiply his pain. 'Shane, come back!' he cries. But the innocence and mythical heroism that *Shane* celebrates was already fading as the western sought to come to terms with a new and complex age. Stevens caught the spirit of an idealized American Dream just in time. He reproduced it majestically.

OPPOSITE, TOP: Shane (Alan Ladd) arrives on horseback at the homestead of Joe Starrett (Van Heflin, offering water).
RIGHT: The evil gunfighter Wilson (Jack Palance) sits tensely in the saloon, waiting for the showdown with Shane.
BOTTOM: One of the homesteaders has been shot by Wilson. His friends gather at the funeral, with Starrett leading them in prayer. Scenes like this emphasize the film's formal lyricism and its response to the splendour of the landscape.
ABOVE: Starrett explains his plans for his place to Shane, whilst his wife Marian (Jean Arthur) looks on. The boy, Joey (Brandon de Wilde) is more interested in Shane's gun and the mystery of Shane's violent past.
LEFT: One of the most poignant farewell scenes in all Westerns, between Shane and Joey. Ironically, there is no room for Shane in the society he has saved and, his job done, he prepares to ride away from the valley.

RIO BRAVO

USA 1959
DIRECTED BY
HOWARD HAWKS

Producer: *Howard Hawks*
Screenplay:
Jules Furthman, Leigh Brackett
From a story by B. H. McCampbell
Music: *Dimitri Tiomkin*
Photography: *Russell Harlan*
Warner Brothers. 141 mins

Leading players:
John Wayne, Dean Martin,
Ricky Nelson, Angie Dickinson,
Walter Brennan, Ward Bond.

The inspiration behind *Rio Bravo* was Howard Hawks's negatiave response to *High Noon*. Was it not ignoble and unprofessional, he thought, for a marshal to go around seeking help for a job he himself had been appointed to do? Unlike Zinnemann's bitter study of individual conscience and communal cowardice, *Rio Bravo* is a droll and relaxed exposition of self-respect and professional teamwork.

As in *High Noon*, the action is concentrated in a single town and pits the forces of law and civilization against a ruthless band of outlaws, whose leader is trying to spring his brother from jail. Sheriff John T. Chance (John Wayne) is massively competent, but, initially, his only helpers are a drunken deputy, Dude (Dean Martin) and a crippled jailer, Stumpy (Walter Brennan). Part of the fun is the irony by which the Sheriff, obstinately refusing help unless it comes up to his own high standards, finds he needs assistance every step of the way. (At one stage he has to be rescued by a deftly directed flower pot.) Chance's heroic example ultimately inspires the others, and yet his stern infallibility is wittily punctured by signs of human vulnerability. This is particularly revealed in his friendship towards Dude and his uneasy emotional involvement with the saloon girl Feathers (Angie Dickinson), a typically forceful Hawksian heroine who refuses to submit to the sheriff's stereotyped judgment of her.

Rio Bravo might seem leisurely, but every scene is relevant to the revelation of character, and the tempo is varied by vivid flurries of action. The almost wordless opening scene that culminates in the brother's arrest for murder is a marvel of economy, revealing the depths to which Dude has sunk. An indication of Dude's former glory is suggested in that brilliant, much imitated bar-room scene when he deduces a murderer's hiding place through spotting drops of blood dripping into a glass. A proficient gunslinger, Colorado (Ricky Nelson), sides with the Sheriff when he blunders into a hold-up attempt, the transformation from helplessness to action – tossing Chance a rifle whilst drawing and using his own gun – performed so rapidly that Hawks can show it within a single frame. Attempting to intimidate Chance and his followers, the outlaws succeed only in steadying their nerve. This stiffening of resolve is conveyed in a gesture: the alcoholic Dude pouring his drink back into the bottle without spilling a drop.

When the Sheriff is asked what he thinks of Colorado as a gunslinger, he replies: 'I'd say he's so good, he doesn't feel he has to prove it.' The film itself has that quality. John Wayne and Dean Martin might seem to be inhabiting familiar roles – authoritarian and alcoholic, respectively – yet the parts are written and conceived so well that neither has ever been better. Hawks never dazzles with his camera (his definition of a good director is: 'Someone who doesn't annoy you'). But the functional, economical style exudes the undemonstrative professionalism he so admires in his characters.

OPPOSITE, TOP: The professionally infallible sheriff (John Wayne) finds he might be romantically susceptible to the saloon girl (Angie Dickinson). The relationship nicely exploits Wayne's uneasiness with women and Hawks's preference for formidable heroines.
BOTTOM: The sheriff's helpers, the crippled Stumpy (Walter Brennan, left) and the drunkard, Dude (Dean Martin, right).
TOP RIGHT: The final shoot-out. Stumpy prepares to toss the dynamite, whilst the sheriff readies himself to shoot it down over the outlaw's lair. Even in this incident, the sheriff needs help, despite his insistence that he does not. The comedy in the scene is typical of Hawks.
BOTTOM RIGHT: The sheriff and his new helper, the gunslinger Colorado (Rick Nelson) have swiftly eliminated some of Burdette's gang, but is Dude safe at the end of the street? This vivid flurry of action has occupied only a few seconds of screen time, a striking contrast to the slow-motion violence of Sam Peckinpah.

THE WILD BUNCH

USA 1969
DIRECTED BY SAM PECKINPAH

Producer: *Phil Feldman*
Screenplay:
Walon Green and Sam Peckinpah
From a story by Walon Green and
Roy N. Sickner
Music: *Jerry Fielding*
Photography: *Lucien Ballard*
Warner Brothers. 145 mins

Leading players:
*William Holden, Ernest Borgnine,
Robert Ryan, Edmond O'Brien,
Warren Oates, Ben Johnson,
Jaime Sanchez, Emilio Fernández.*

ABOVE: The Wild Bunch. LEFT: the Bunch's leader, Pike Bishop (William Holden). 'We've got to start thinking beyond our guns,' he will say. 'Those days are closin' fast.' BELOW: The two Gorch brothers (Warren Oates, left and Ben Johnson, right) take a shower of booze with the girls. CENTRE: A remarkable high-angle shot of the opening massacre in the town, when the Bunch's attempted bank robbery goes violently wrong. RIGHT: Dutch (Ernest Borgnine) comes to the aid of Bishop in the final gunfight. BOTTOM RIGHT: Once a close friend of Bishop, Deke Thornton (Robert Ryan, on horseback) rounds up his posse to continue the pursuit of the Wild Bunch after the failure of their attempted ambush in the town. *The Wild Bunch* brought madness and extremes of violence to the Western. We have come a long way from *Stagecoach*. Nevertheless, the film won great acclaim and even inspired a symphony (John McCabe's 2nd).

'What is the motivation of a man who becomes a professional soldier or an outlaw? I believe it is most always a love of violence,' said director Sam Peckinpah. Of all his films, *The Wild Bunch* is the one most deeply obsessed by this proposition. The Wild Bunch themselves are outlaws committed to asserting themselves through action and aggression. We follow them from a bungled bank robbery, which erupts into sickeningly indiscriminate slaughter, to their deaths at the hands of the Mexican army, which becomes a hideously prolonged ballet of choreographed carnage. In the process, we watch also the pieties of the traditional western – of sanitized violence and simplistic distinctions between good and evil – being torn apart.

The Wild Bunch marks the definitive ending of the 'noble' western. Its savagery of language and action brings a new harshness to a genre that has until then

been predominantly elegiac and idealistic. The new permissiveness of the cinema seemed to demand a correspondingly tougher depiction of the West, in which the outlaw is de-romanticized and the violence is painful. In the context of the Vietnam war also, it may well be that Sam Peckinpah felt unable to celebrate American adventurism and swaggering self-assertion with the usual uncomplicated vigour. The film is deeply ambivalent about its heroes, taking their actions to mad and venomous extremes. They are aggressive anachronisms, yet they also represent a vitality and individualism that, during the action of the film, is being lost in the encroachment of civilization and the closing of the frontier.

The tone is set by that extraordinary opening, where some children (the future) watch as a scorpion (the Wild Bunch) is devoured by hordes of ants (the modern world). The modern world has entered the western. One could see *The Wild Bunch* as a prolonged revenge on western myths, in which children are now implicated in the violence (compare the innocence of the child in *Shane*) and women who have frequently been ignored or abused in the genre now begin to strike back. For some it was just too extreme, deliberate and self-conscious. ('O hell,' said Howard Hawks about Peckinpah, 'I can kill five guys and have 'em buried in the time it takes him to kill one.') But, for most people, with its ferocious statement about violence as the American way of life, *The*

Wild Bunch revitalized the relevance of the western as a genre.

Peckinpah is the true descendant of John Ford. There is sometimes great lyricism and tenderness in his work (seen here in the beautifully filmed departure of the Wild Bunch from the Mexican village), a similarly resplendent visual sense, and a raucous male humour. But whereas the classicist Ford brings out the poetry in the legends of the American pioneering past, the modernist Peckinpah is more likely to explore its passions and perversions. 'When the legend becomes fact, print the legend,' may have been Ford's thought. 'Print the fact,' may be Peckinpah's. The realism of *The Wild Bunch* is red-raw and, after it, the western could never be – and has never been – the same.

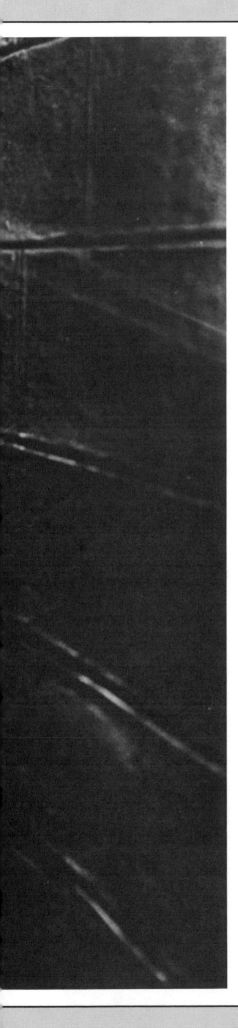

COMEDY

City Lights (1931) · *A Night At The Opera* (1935) ·
All About Eve (1950) · *Mon Oncle* (1958) ·
Some Like It Hot (1959)

Film comedy has produced a number of remarkable performer-directors. Two
of the greatest where Charles Chaplin and Jacques Tati. LEFT: Chaplin in
solitary pose in *City Lights*.
ABOVE: Jacques Tati seen as Monsieur Hulot in his sister's ghastly, ultra-
modern garden in *Mon Oncle*.

CITY LIGHTS

USA 1931
DIRECTED BY
CHARLES CHAPLIN

Producer: *Charles Chaplin*
Screenplay: *Charles Chaplin*
Photography: *Rollie Totheroh,
Gordon Pollock, Mark Marlatt*
United Artists. 87 mins

Leading players:
*Charles Chaplin,
Virginia Cherrill, Harry Myers.*

Woody Allen's favourite screen comedy is, apparently, *City Lights*, and he prefers Chaplin to Keaton because 'Chaplin took risks'. The risk Chaplin took in *City Lights* was to turn his back on the talkies. It was still possible, he believed, to elicit humour and pathos through mime. His decision was triumphantly vindicated. As always, Chaplin only got into trouble when he opened his mouth – in life, as in his films.

City Lights was not completely silent, of course. Chaplin added music, which typically underscored the story's sentiment rather than its humour. He also made comic use of sound, like that moment at a rich man's party when Charlie swallows a toy whistle and develops a shrill hiccough, disrupting a musical performance and accidentally summoning the neighbourhood dogs. Mostly the comedy resides in Chaplin's physical dexterity and pantomime eloquence. His elaborate soft-shoe

shuffle to evade a massive boxer, whom he is fighting to raise money, is a particular highlight.

The dramatic situation of *City Lights* is one of Chaplin's neatest. Charlie has saved a drunken millionaire (Harry Myers) from drowning. When the rich man is intoxicated, he treats Charlie like a prince, showering him with money, which Charlie donates towards an eventually successful eye operation for a blind flower seller (Virginia Cherrill) whom he loves. When the millionaire is sober, he sees Charlie as an objectionable tramp and treats him abominably, finally accusing him of theft and having him sent to prison.

The whole film is about different kinds of social blindness. Because she cannot see his shabby appearance, the flower-girl is not prejudiced against Charlie, but she imagines his generosity must stem from a privileged social standing. When sober, what irritates the millionaire about Charlie is his independence of spirit, possibly recognizing a side of himself he had to drive out to get rich. The millionaire's sober side presents a remarkably cruel, uncaring image of material success. When drunk, he and Charlie are as close as King Lear and his Fool.

At the end of the film, Charlie passes a flower shop which the girl, whose sight has been restored, now owns. Patronizingly, she offers him a flower. Recognition dawns when their hands touch. She is startled to see for the first time the identity of her benefactor, and the film closes with a close-up of Charlie at this point of recognition – apologetic, delighted, wondering what she is thinking and, through her, unnervingly seeing *himself* for the first time.

Chaplin had a simple technical rule: long-shot for comedy, close-up for tragedy. In its exploration of the connection between love and sacrifice and the conflict between rich and poor, *City Lights* is a tragedy of sorts, foreshadowing some of the darker implications of later Chaplin. Some observers dislike the Dickensian sentimentalities and socialist sympathies in Chaplin. But, as James Agee wisely said, Chaplin was the artist who, of all comedians, 'worked most deeply and most shrewdly within a realization of what a human being is, and is up against'. For Chaplin, it was not enough to be merely the greatest clown of screen comedy; he insisted also on being its social conscience. He fulfilled that role incomparably.

OPPOSITE, TOP: Charlie buys a flower from the blind girl (Virginia Cherill), who mistakes him for a rich man.

CENTRE: Charlie obtains a job as a road-sweeper. Here he is dismayed to see additional work being provided by an approaching elephant.

BOTTOM: Visiting the girl in her home, Charlie tries to play the part of a gentleman. He learns that the girl and her grandmother are due to be evicted because they cannot pay the rent.

TOP: Charlie with the drunken millionaire (Harry Myers), whom he has saved from committing suicide. 'Be brave! Face life!' advises Charlie.

ABOVE: The millionaire takes his new friend to an expensive restaurant, where Charlie confuses the confetti with the spaghetti.

RIGHT: In order to raise money to pay the girl's rent, Charlie becomes a boxer for the night and has to take on a tough opponent (Hank Mann). Here he is taking refuge behind the referee.

A Night At The Opera

USA 1935
Directed by Sam Wood

Producer: *Irving G. Thalberg*
Screenplay: *George S. Kaufman
and Morrie Ryskind.*
From a story by
James Kevin McGuinness
Music: *Herbert Stothart*
Photography: *Merritt B. Gerstad*
MGM. 94 mins

Leading players:
*Groucho Marx, Chico Marx,
Harpo Marx, Margaret Dumont,
Allan Jones, Kitty Carlisle,
Sig Rumann.*

If Chaplin represented the social conscience of screen comedy, the Marx Brothers were its great anarchists, a deadly trio that routed their adversaries either through withering wit (Groucho) cute conmanship (Chico) or mute mania (Harpo). Their speciality was the mutilation of sacred cows, whether these took the form of womanhood (generally represented by that most beloved of sacred cows, Margaret Dumont), political statesmanship, higher education or even higher culture.

A *Night at the Opera* sees the Marx Brothers at pretty nearly their peak. It is certainly their last great film. After this, by extending the romantic and musical interludes between the clowning, Hollywood studios attempted to broaden their appeal by making them more endearing to women, who, it was felt, found them misogynistic and even downright alarming. The result tended towards a disappointing comic slackness.

Even in A *Night at the Opera*, the romantic sub-plot is heavy going unless one is prepared to take it in the wrong spirit and make it part of the hilarity, which is not hard to do. The boys are called upon to help the prima donna Rosa (Kitty Carlisle) fend off the attentions of the esteemed tenor Lasparri (Walter King) and encourage the singing ambitions of her true love, Ricardo (Allen Jones). Fortunately this re-routing of the course of true love takes up little of the boys' time as it is crosscut with Otis B. Driftwood's less than sincere attempts to introduce Mrs Claypole (Margaret Dumont) into high society by making her a patroness of the opera.

The comic routines are some of the finest ever devised for them. Groucho's ever-more-crowded cabin finally explodes people into the corridor when Margaret Dumont opens the door. An ingenious game of hotel beds is played with an ingenuous plain-clothes detective ('You look more like an old clothes detective to me,' says Groucho), in which the beds keep disappearing under the detective's nose. Verdi's *Il Trovatore* is well and truly murdered through the boys' high jinks, which incorporate Groucho's irreverent attitude to the arts ('How would you like to feel the way she looks?' he says of one straining soprano) and which include one

astounding shot of Harpo's slitting a theatrical backdrop clean down the middle as he falls spectacularly to the stage.

There is a particularly brilliant exchange between Groucho and Chico as, between them, they systematically shred a complicated contract. The last part to go is a 'sanity clause' because of Chico's insistence that: 'There ain't no Sanity Clause'. In the best Marx Brothers films, there is no sanity clause. For most of its length, A *Night at the Opera* is delirious, uninhibited, insane Marxism.

BOTTOM LEFT: When Margaret Dumont opens the door, Groucho and numerous occupants of his overcrowded 'stateroom' explode into the corridor.
LEFT: Chico (left), Allan Jones (centre) and Harpo (right) disguise themselves as Russian aviators in order to disembark.
CENTRE: Chico, Harpo and Allan Jones entertain themselves, whilst Mr Gottlieb, director of the New York Opera Company (Sig Rumann, left) fumes with rage. Groucho (right) lounges, unconcerned.
RIGHT: Harpo disrupts the performance of the opera by sliding down the middle of a theatrical backdrop, slicing it in two.
BOTTOM RIGHT: The final scene. The two young principals (Kitty Carlisle and Allan Jones, left) have rescued the opera, but Mr Gottlieb still feels it necessary to chastise Groucho. Chico and Harpo are in attendance, Margaret Dumont looks on proudly, now established as patroness of the arts. All New York will be at her feet. 'There's plenty of room,' says Groucho.

ALL ABOUT EVE

USA 1950

DIRECTED BY
JOSEPH L. MANKIEWICZ

Producer: *Darryl F. Zanuck*
Screenplay: *Joseph L. Mankiewicz*
Music: *Alfred Newman*
Photography: *Milton Krasner*
20th Century-Fox. 130 mins

Leading players:
*Bette Davis, Anne Baxter,
George Sanders, Celeste Holm,
Gary Merrill, Hugh Marlowe,
Thelma Ritter, Marilyn Monroe,
Barbara Bates.*

The theme of Joseph L. Mankiewicz's *All About Eve* is: there's no bitchiness like show bitchiness. Eve Harrington (Anne Baxter) is a predatory stage actress who will do anything to further her career. Symbolizing the infinite resources of feminine guile ('male behaviour is so elementary,' said Mankiewicz, 'that *All About Adam* could be done as a short'), Eve is also a metaphor for the kind of naked ambition that exists in any competitive strata of society in which ends justify means: the higher the stakes, the lower the behaviour. The film is all about evil; also, all about ego.

'You gather I don't like Eve,' said Mankiewicz. 'You're right. I've been there.' A veteran of Hollywood, who had made such elegant and literary films as *A Letter to Three Wives* (1949) and *Five Fingers* (1952), Mankiewicz knew all about conspiracy and the thirst for success. The characters seem vividly drawn from experience – the ruthless aspirant, Eve, with youth on her side; the temperamental star, Margo (Bette Davis), who fears age and loneliness waiting in the wings; and the suave critic, Addison DeWitt (George Sanders) whose willingness to wound reflects an arid contempt for humanity.

Mankiewicz dissects the foibles of his characters with a detached and cynical disdain. Eve's fabricated tale of hardship at the beginning absolutely entrances the theatre people, who can no longer differentiate truth from a great performance. When angry, Margo uses language as poisoned darts of wounded ego. 'Fasten your seat belts,' she says, limbering up like a prize-fighter for her party, 'it's gonna be a bumpy night.' Addison practises man-

oueuvres. 'That's Max Fabian, the producer, dear,' he says to a young starlet (Marilyn Monroe). 'Now go and do yourself some good.'

It is a cleverly constructed film, beginning with Eve's acceptance of a top theatrical award and then, in flashback, revealing the labyrinthine progress by which she won it. Past and present coalesce when an aspiring young actress visits Eve in her apartment, which recalls the way the main plot started. The last shot shows the girl (Barbara Bates) as she poses in front of a mirror with Eve's dress and award, a reminder of a key moment earlier when Margo has discovered Eve doing precisely that, and a shot which, with its infinite mirror reflections, suggests a multiplicity of Eves spreading in our society.

Although (Eve-like) Bette Davis only landed the role of Margo when the original choice, Claudette Colbert, was injured, she is magnificent, not so much declaiming as detonating her lines, and yet conveying the woman behind the actress with great sympathy. Sanders understandably purrs through his dialogue – he has never had it so good. Even the asides sparkle: like the moment at the party when Birdie (the irreplaceable Thelma Ritter) sees the fur coats splayed out and remarks that 'the bed looks like a dead animal act'; or that revealing slip, when, accidentally or calculatedly, Margo refers to Eve as 'Miss Worthington' – the daughter who should not be put on the stage. The epigrammatic wit and waspish wisdom of *All About Eve* belong to a lost era of Hollywood comedy when eloquence was golden.

TOP LEFT: Ambitious stage actresss, Eve Harrington (Anne Baxter, right) confronts a young admirer (Barbara Bates).
LEFT: The star in her dressing room. Margo Channing (Bette Davis) talks to her closest friends; her dresser, Birdie (Thelma Ritter, standing), the writer, Lloyd Richards (Hugh Marlowe, in chair) and the writer's wife, Karen (Celeste Holm, in fur coat).
TOP RIGHT: Eve meets the powerful critic, Addison DeWitt (George Sanders, right), watched disdainfully by Margo and innocently by Addison's companion, Miss Casswell (Marilyn Monroe).
CENTRE RIGHT: Karen looks shifty – she is sabotaging Margo's drive back to the theatre, in order to give Eve her big break. Her husband (Hugh Marlowe) is the unsuspecting driver whose gasoline tank has been emptied.
FAR RIGHT: When friendly persuasion fails, Eve threatens to blackmail Karen in order to secure the lead in her husband's play.
BOTTOM RIGHT: Margo congratulates Eve on her Sarah Siddons Award. Director Bill Sampson (Gary Merill), relishes the irony of the scene.

MON ONCLE

FRANCE 1958
DIRECTED BY JACQUES TATI

Screenplay: *Jacques Tati
and Jacques Legrange*
Music: *Alain Romans*
Photography: *Jean Bourgoin*
116 mins

Leading players:
*Jacques Tati, Jean-Pierre Zola,
Adrienne Servantie.*

As Monsieur Hulot, with his shrunken raincoat, cockeyed pipe, redundant stick and oddly elongated walk, Jacques Tati was the greatest silent comedian of the sound era. Yet, if not verbal, his comedy was often aural, the soundtrack of clicks, squeaks and roars a satirical commentary on the cacophonous non-communication of modern life.

As a director, Tati favoured contemplative long shots, with an acute attention to detail in the foreground and background. He very rarely used a close-up for effect for, as he said, 'in real life, we don't stand on top of people's noses'. He never harangued or cajoled an audience: he invited them into his world. What, then, was the essence of his comedy? Jean-Luc Godard nicely characterized it as Tati's 'feeling for strangeness'. Tati could point his camera in such a way as to make modern society look like science-fiction.

Mon Oncle is basically a tale of two homes. Hulot lives at the top of a winding apartment block in the old quarter of town. His sister and brother-in-law, the Arpels, live in a suburban house that is the ultimate in automation. Hulot's surroundings are messy but they breathe life. The Arpels's home is a study in plastic, regulated, quite dead. Hulot's young nephew seems instinctively drawn to the warmth and vitality of Hulot's environment rather than to that of his parents, where all is sanitized to extinction.

A slim plot builds when Hulot goes to work, disastrously, at his brother-in-law's plastics works. Mostly the film is a comic elaboration of the contrast between the natural and the mechanical. Hulot adjusts his window so that the sunlight can shine on a bird on the ledge below, and the bird

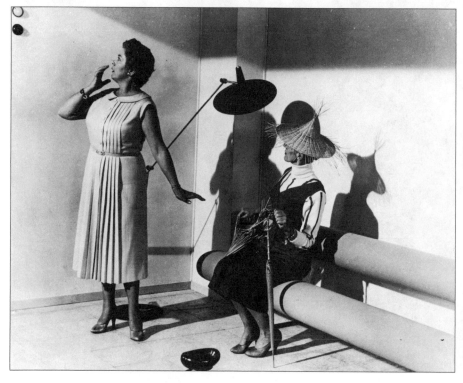

gratefully starts to sing. In contrast, his sister has a mechanical fish in her garden that spouts water at the flick of a switch. The joke is repeated so often that it ceases to be funny and becomes a portrait of a character whose reactions and routines are becoming as automatic as the objects with which she surrounds herself. Even the animals show more life than the humans. A dog at Hulot's local market barks manically at a dead fish protruding from a shopping basket. The joke anticipates that moment when the Arpels's dog inadvertently locks its dead-fish owners in their automated garage through straying across the electric eye; precision technology suddenly defeated by canine unpredictability.

As well as a film about automation, *Mon Oncle* is a film about appearances. Madame Arpel is so obsessed with appearance that she will brush a single leaf off her spotless path, whilst Hulot is so confused by appearance that he mistakes the new outfit of his sister's neighbour for a carpet-seller's wares. During such blunders, Hulot remains serene and decorous at all times, which adds to the fun. But his gestures can also seem old-fashioned and futile (for example, when he replaces a brick on an already crumbling wall), which adds to the sadness. Behind the comedy, there is a characteristic Tati-esque warning that this enveloping environmental mechanization could lead to emotional sterility.

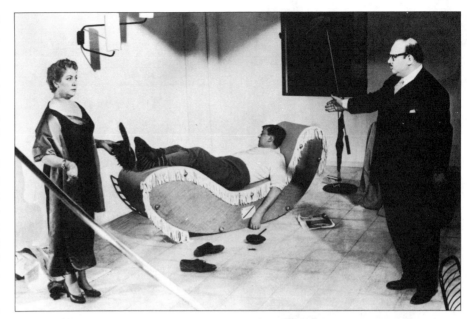

Mon Oncle won the Oscar as the best foreign film of 1958. It is the most Chaplinesque of Tati's comedies, like *Modern Times* showing the hero at odds with technological, automated society. Yet, paradoxically, Tati is the coolest, most mathematically precise of comedy directors.
OPPOSITE, TOP: Monsieur Hulot with his nephew, who finds Hulot a far more congenial character than his parents.
BOTTOM LEFT: Madame Arpel and her neighbour. The similarity between the lampshade and the neighbour's hat, both symmetrically framed by shadow, shows Tati's eye for weird visual puns.
TOP RIGHT: Monsieur Hulot slouches untidily in Madame Arpel's immaculate house, to the disapproval of his sister and brother-in-law.
RIGHT: Hulot and a guest perform an involuntary two-step whilst negotiating the stepping stones.
BOTTOM: Hulot at Madame Arpel's sedate garden party, which he is destined to disrupt when he attempts to repair the fountain.

SOME LIKE IT HOT

USA 1959
DIRECTED BY BILLY WILDER

Producer: *Billy Wilder*
Screenplay: *Billy Wilder and
I. A. L. Diamond*
Music: *Adolph Deutsch*
Photography: *Charles Lang Jr*
United Artists. 121 mins

Leading players:
*Marilyn Monroe, Tony Curtis,
Jack Lemmon, George Raft,
Joe E. Brown, Pat O'Brien.*

In *Some Like it Hot*, two jazz musicians inadvertently witness the St Valentine's Day Massacre and disguise themselves as members of an all-girl band to escape from Chicago to Florida. Fainter hearts might think twice about the humorous potential of murder and transvestism. Billy Wilder's film triumphs because the counterpoint between the farcical foreground (the disguise) and the brutal background (the pursuing gangsters) gives a rare energy and excitement to the humour. Comedy is often at its best when it is about the extremities of survival.

The film exuberantly evokes the period. In Wilder's hands, the Twenties really roar, with flappers, gangsters, syncopated jazz, tangos, and gin flasks hidden in garters as a reminder of the prohibitions of Prohibition. The stylized setting keeps the violence at arm's length, and uncomfortable realism is offset still further by allusions to past movies. The glittering monochrome photography evokes the classic gangster era, as does George Raft as he snaps at a coin-tossing hood (a reference to *Scarface*) and threatens one of his boys with a grapefruit (a reference to *Public Enemy*).

'We're the new girls,' says Tony Curtis when introducing himself to the band, to which Jack Lemmon adds, with what sounds like relish: '*Brand* new.' Lemmon's gloriously unzipped performance shows an inhibited man finding a new lease of life in this role: released from macho pressures, he enjoys being a girl. As a new girl, the lecherous Curtis discovers how the other half lives, which is to modify his previously callous treatment of women as sex objects. Curtis has been courting the lead singer, Sugar (Marilyn Monroe), in another disguise as an impotent, myopic millionaire with a voice like Cary Grant. Towards the end he is to risk his life apologising to her ('None of that, Sugar, no guy is worth it'), giving a stunned Monroe a big sloppy kiss while still wearing his drag wig. As the alcoholic romantic and sexual victim who is almost through with love, Marilyn Monroe gives a performance which at the time looked delightful and, in retrospect, has a moving poignancy.

Wilder winds the film up like a coiled spring, propelling it with such slickness, pace and conviction that one scarcely has time to take breath. Although seeming to grow wilder and wilder, the film has an unerring structural logic. When we think we have moved a long way from St Valentine's Day, and Chicago, a single image – Lemmon's double-bass riddled with bullet holes – can thrust the threat to the forefront of our minds. At the end, the musicians are once again being pursued, with Curtis having a forgiving Monroe in tow, and a bewigged Lemmon trying to explain the impossibility of marriage to his love-smitten millionaire (Joe E. Brown). 'Oh, you don't understand, Osgood!' he says, and takes off his wig. 'I'm a man!' To which his partner replies, unfazed: 'Well, nobody's perfect.' For perfection in screen humour, look no farther than *Some Like it Hot*, the last comedy classic of Hollywood's golden years.

TOP LEFT: 'We're the new girls. . .' Disguised as Josephine (Tony Curtis, left) and Daphne (Jack Lemon, right), Joe and Gerry attempt to make their getaway from Chicago.

LEFT: The new girls meet the lead singer of Sweet Sue's Society Syncopaters, Sugar Kane (Marilyn Monroe).

BELOW: A frisky millionaire (Joe E. Brown) takes a fancy to Daphne (Jack Lemmon). 'I'm Osgood Fielding the Third,' he says, when helping Daphne with her shoe. 'I'm Cinderella the Second,' snaps Daphne.

RIGHT: The band rehearses. Josephine plays a mean saxophone, Daphne thwacks a maternal double bass and Sugar plucks a fragile ukelele.

BOTTOM RIGHT: Daphne points accusingly at the millionaire talking to Sugar, whom he recognizes as Joe in disguise. Notice how Joe is clutching his basket of shells; it reminds him, he tells Sugar, of the company he owns. 'Shell Oil?!' she exclaims. 'Please – no names,' he replies.

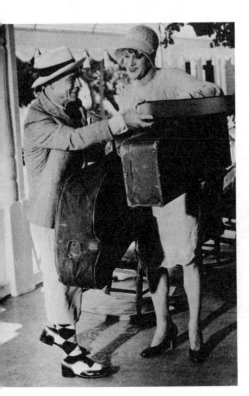

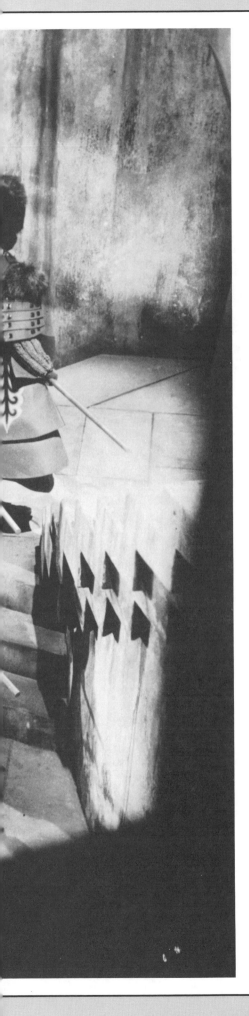

MUSICALS

42nd Street (1933) · *The Wizard of Oz* (1939) ·
Singin' in the Rain (1952) · *Funny Face* (1956) ·
The Sound of Music (1965)

Joy, fantasy and energy are at the heart of the great musicals.
LEFT: Judy Garland and her friends are taken prisoner in one of the great
fantasy-musicals, *The Wizard of Oz*.
ABOVE: Audrey Hepburn lets her hair down in a Parisian night club in *Funny
Face*, watched by Fred Astaire.

42ND STREET

USA 1933
DIRECTED BY LLOYD BACON

Producer: *Hal B. Wallis*
Screenplay: *James Seymour,*
Rian James
Based on the novel by
Bradford Ropes
Music: *Al Dubin and Harry Warren*
Photography: *Sol Polito*
Choreography: *Busby Berkeley*
Warner Brothers. 89 mins

Leading players:
Warner Baxter, Ruby Keeler,
Bebe Daniels, Dick Powell,
George Brent, Ginger Rogers.

42nd Street is the archetypal backstage musical, with hitches both technical and temperamental, and in which a frenzied director has to say to his untried leading lady: 'You're going out a youngster – but you've *gotta* come back a star!' About putting on a show, *42nd Street* puts on quite a show itself.

Like many Warner Brothers musicals of the Thirties (and unlike those made at Paramount and MGM), the film is initially characterized by its realism. Depression is in the air, the style is slick and tough, the milieu urban and working class. The chorus girls are a notably hard-headed bunch, with a keen sense of rivalry, a cynicism about sex, and a resilient and waspish humour. Ginger Rogers plays a girl called 'Anytime Annie' of whom one girl comments: 'She only said "No" once – and then she didn't hear the question.' When the dewy-eyed heroine (Ruby

Keeler) is introduced, her simplicity of heart is received with amused incredulity by the girls. 'You can't be only eighteen,' says one, 'a girl couldn't get that dumb in only eighteen years.'

Miss Keeler gets her break (literally, when the star, Bebe Daniels, breaks her ankle), but her success is the result not of luck but of effort. This is the Warner's version of the American Dream: everything comes to him (or her) who *works*. She also succeeds because of the dedication and obsession of the director (an intense performance from Warner Baxter), an effort which leaves him exhausted in the film's subdued finale. Through him, the film becomes a thoughtful study of the knife-edge between success and failure, in which team effort, under enlightened guidance, can make all the difference. Maybe a message for the times. The director copes with and conquers his depression: *the* Depression might be similarly overcome.

As the film develops, choreographer Busby Berkeley comes into his own. He imposes his own unique geometry, both erotic and aesthetic, on numbers such as 'Young and Healthy', 'Shuffle off to Buffalo' and the title number, which incorporates street violence, stylized sets and a dazzling tap routine by Ruby Keeler on the top of a taxi. In recent years, there has been a tendency to liken Busby Berkeley's procedures to the Nazi propaganda films of Leni Riefenstahl: young

people being moulded into a single shape and entity by the will of one man. (Clive James referred to Berkeley's routines as 'looking like colonies of bacteria staging a political rally under a microscope'.) But to accuse Berkeley of choreographic Fascism seems absurd. If anything, the political implication of his method is quite the reverse. His patterns suggest that everyone has an equally important part to play if the enterprise is to achieve a harmonious whole. That it does achieve this is a tribute to the willingness of people to work together. The show is a triumph of teamwork, and so is the film. Depression audiences must have found comfort in the message.

ABOVE LEFT: The girls arrive for rehearsal, preparing for hours of gruelling work. Ruby Keeler is third from left, Una Merkel is centre, and Ginger Rogers holds the dog.
ABOVE: Hard at it, the girls are put through their paces. Ginger Rogers is wearing the monocle; on her left are Ruby Keeler and Una Merkel.
TOP RIGHT: The star of the show (Bebe Daniels, seated on a park bench) argues with her lover (George Brent). One of the few moments when the action goes outdoors.
FAR RIGHT: The director, Julian Marsh (Warner Baxter), reprimands his young hopeful (Ruby Keeler): Una Merkel and Ginger Rogers look on. Baxter's director represents the dedication necessary for any show to succeed, and the actor's performance gives the film much of its drive and tension.
RIGHT: A number from the show itself. Keeler dances amid the skyscrapers of New York. It is here that Busby Berkeley's exuberant choreography comes into its own.

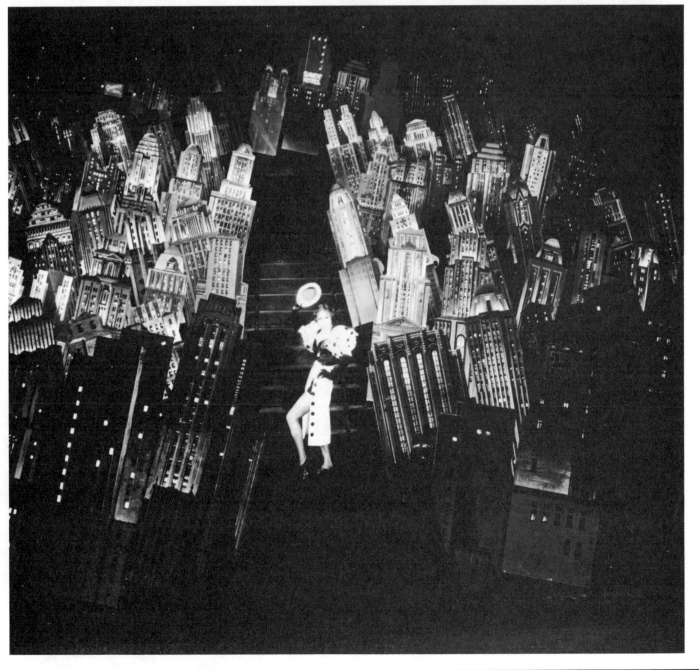

THE WIZARD OF OZ

USA 1939

DIRECTED BY VICTOR FLEMING

Producer: *Mervyn LeRoy*
Screenplay: *Noel Langley,*
Florence Ryerson,
Edgar Allan Wolfe
From the novel by Frank L. Baum
Songs: *E. Y. Harburg and*
Harold Arlen
Photography: *Harold Rosson*
MGM. 102 mins

Leading players:
Judy Garland, Ray Bolger,
Jack Haley, Bert Lahr,
Margaret Hamilton, Billie Burke,
Frank Morgan

TOP LEFT: Dorothy (Judy Garland) pleads on behalf of her dog to her aunt (Clara Bandick, seated). On Dorothy's left is the querulous neighbour (Margaret Hamilton) who is to be transformed by Dorothy's imagination into the Wicked Witch. Dorothy's uncle (Charley Grapewin) looks on. LEFT: Now stranded in her fantasy land, Dorothy meets the Scarecrow (Ray Bolger). BELOW: 'Ding Dong! The Witch is dead!' Accidentally sprinkled by water, the Witch (Margaret Hamilton) screams and writhes as she begins to diminish before the astonished eyes of the Lion (Bert Lahr), the Tin Man (Jack Haley) and the Scarecrow (Ray Bolger). TOP RIGHT: Dorothy and Toto in Wonderland, and over the rainbow. FAR RIGHT: 'We're off to see the Wizard': the Lion, Dorothy, the Tin Man and the Scarecrow follow the yellow brick road to meet the Wizard who can solve all their problems.

The Wizard of Oz is the American *Alice in Wonderland*, taking us not down the rabbit-hole but over the rainbow. It roams the often fearful world of dream and imagination, in which the recognizable is distorted into fanciful shapes, before concluding, reassuringly, that home is best. Frank Baum's story had been filmed twice before but, as with other frequently filmed tales such as *The Prisoner of Zenda* and *The Maltese Falcon*, for most people there is only one classic version that lives in the memory. *The Wizard of Oz* means, basically, Judy Garland in her ruby slippers, sparkling songs, and Technicolor of a garishness that could only exist in someone's mind rather than in someone's house. It is the definitive film pantomime.

Children love it because it does not talk down to them. (In fact, according to Graham Greene, the British Board of Film Censors in 1939 found the film frightening enough to give it a certificate for adults only.) The film's fantasy is not charming and fey, but imaginatively credible in its own terms and sometimes spooky. The tornado which signals the transition from sepia reality in Kansas to colourful unreality in Oz is vividly done. And the cast inhabit their roles with the utmost conviction. Ray Bolger as the 'brainless' Scarecrow, Jack Haley as the 'heartless' Tin Man, and Bert Lahr as the 'gutless' Lion never did anything more memorable on film, whilst Magaret Hamilton as the Wicked Witch has features so extraordinarily sharp that she looks like a line drawing of flinty evil. As Dorothy, Judy Garland projects the ideal blend of earnest sincerity and unsentimental wonder.

It is strange to recall now that Garland only secured the role when Darryl Zanuck refused to lend Shirley Temple to MGM – 'thus doing the world an enduring favour', as David Shipman wisely remarked. There was also considerable debate over whether to retain her big song, 'Over the Rainbow' in the final film, this scene actually being filmed by King Vidor when the assigned director, Victor Fleming, left prematurely to take over the reigns of *Gone With the Wind* from George Cukor, who reputedly had incurred the displeasure of Clark Gable. Such eccentric manoeuvres might have disrupted the unity and teamwork of a lesser production, but everything in this film seems touched by a magic wand. It ushered in a decade and a half of great MGM musicals. It is hard to conceive of any succeeding generation that would not respond with delight to the Good Witch's appeal to 'Follow the Yellow Brick Road'.

SINGIN' IN THE RAIN

USA 1952
DIRECTED BY GENE KELLY AND STANLEY DONEN

Producer: *Arthur Freed*
Screenplay: *Betty Comden and Adolph Green*
Songs: *Arthur Freed and Nacio Herb Brown, Betty Comden, Adolph Green and Roger Edens*
Photography: *Harold Rosson*
MGM. 103 mins

Leading players:
Gene Kelly, Donald O'Connor, Debbie Reynolds, Jean Hagen, Millard Mitchell, Cyd Charisse.

Indisputably one of the greatest of film musicals, *Singin' In the Rain* has not had sufficient credit as probably the screen's most brilliant comedy about the film industry. Disastrous sneak previews, fickle fans, scatty columnists, maniacal directors and an awesomely untalented star who believes her own publicity are only some of the creations of a delectable screenplay from writers who know this crazy world from the inside and are still sane enough to see its funny side.

The humour and invention carry over into the musical numbers, which are steeped in movie mythology, including a spectacular parody of Busby Berkeley's unique brand of formation dancing (*Beautiful Girl*), a take-off of the gangster film with a scar-faced hoodlum who obsessively tosses a coin, and a serenade ('You were meant for me') where the hero needs the props of a sound stage to make his romantic overtures sound convincing.

Practically every form of Hollywood entertainment – costume drama, silent western, screwball comedy – is incorporated into this niftily nostalgic look at the traumas and triumphs of Hollywood's transition to sound in 1929.

The hero, Don Lockwood (Gene Kelly), is a silent film star whose career is momentarily disrupted by the coming of talkies but also by the criticism of a young showgirl Kathy (Debbie Reynolds) who dismisses his performances as 'dumb show'. Of course, he and Kathy are to fall in love, and his ecstasy is to overflow into the immortal 'Singin' in the Rain' routine, which is the most exhilarating display of *joie de vivre* in the history of the film musical and the masterpiece of Gene Kelly's many superlative contributions to the genre as performer, choreographer and director. But the number also works brilliantly because of its precise integration into the whole context of the film. It is the

moment when Lockwood celebrates not only love but self-recognition: his acknowledgment that he is a music man, not an actor. The number is a glorious sudden discovery of professional self-respect; it washes Lockwood clean.

Explicitly the film is showing how Hollywood came to terms with sound; co-operative and creative inventiveness adjusted to technological invention. Implicitly it is a similarly ringing declaration of confidence in Hollywood's capacity to absorb a new technological threat in the 1950s – television. It might be thought to be simply putting a brave face on the situation – singin' in the rain, in fact. In retrospect, however, the film's exuberance and quality have a point to make. At the time, *Singin' in the Rain* was greeted rather complacently as just another example of the sort of thing Hollywood does rather well. Its only significant Oscar nomination went to Jean Hagen for her hilarious supporting performance as the squeaky siren, Lina Lamont. More recently, a poll of international film critics voted it the third best film ever made. As François Truffaut remarked, nowadays it is one of those films that contrasts so sharply with the insipidity of television that it could never look old-fashioned. It might be MGM's love song to itself, but no film does more credit to the essence of MGM escapist entertainment than *Singin' In the Rain*.

OPPOSITE: 'Gotta dance!' During his fantasy ballet, Don Lockwood (Gene Kelly) encounters a gangster's seductive moll (Cyd Charisse, with leg outstretched). BOTTOM LEFT: The ecstasy of love and self-fulfilment: Gene Kelly dances round the lamp post whilst Singin' in the Rain. This deceptively simple and flawlessly executed number has become a cinema classic. RIGHT: 'Good Morning!' Donald O'Connor, Debbie Reynolds and Gene Kelly have the idea of transforming *The Duelling Cavalier* into a musical. BELOW: Coming to terms with sound. The director (Douglas Fowley) shows where he will place the microphone to his apprehensive stars, Lockwood (Gene Kelly) and Lina Lamont (Jean Hagen). Miss Lamont's vocal coach (Kathleen Freeman) looks on imperiously. Miss Lamont will later exlaim: 'I can't make love to a *bush!*' BOTTOM RIGHT: 'Gotta Dance! Gotta Dance!' Gene Kelly and cast in the 'Broadway Melody' routine.

51

FUNNY FACE

USA 1956
DIRECTED BY STANLEY DONEN

PRODUCER: *Roger Edens*
Screenplay: *Leonard Gershe*
Songs: *George and Ira Gershwin.*
Additional songs by
Roger Edens and Leonard Gershe
Music conducted by
Adolph Deutsch
Photography: *Ray June*
Paramount. 103 mins

Leading players:
*Audrey Hepburn, Fred Astaire,
Kay Thompson, Robert Flemyng,
Michel Auclair.*

A celebration of song and dance on celluloid would be unthinkable without Fred Astaire and, although other films might have been more spectacular examples of his prowess, he has never made a better musical than *Funny Face*. He plays a fashion magazine photographer who, searching for a girl with a new look, a 'funny face', becomes entranced by a bookshop assistant (Audrey Hepburn). Unfortunately, she is more interested in philosophy than photography. However, tempted by the offer of a trip to Paris where she can meet her philosopher hero Émile Flostre (Michel Auclair), she agrees to model the new outfits.

Because the film was about fashion photography, director Stanley Donen was determined to give the film a stunning look. Dazzling pinks for 'Think Pink', red filters for 'Funny Face', an overhead shot of a swirling multi-coloured hat and veil in 'How long has this been going on?', portraits of Hepburn in Paris broken down through their primary colours to black-and-white before recolouring – the film is a feast for the eyes. It also has tremendous stylistic panache. The dialogue delivery has rhythm as well as pace, and the numbers work like a charm because they do not interrupt but actually further narrative and character. 'Bonjour Paris!', with its spanking rhythm, dashing split-screen, and vivid response to place, is a number bubbling over with exhilaration and joy.

Colour and choreography are augmented by a rich vein of comedy, often musical. The lyrics mischievously rhyme 'Montmartre' with 'Jean-Paul Sartre', and a pompous fanfare for the fashion show discovers a wonderfully incongruous link between the opening bars of Gershwin's 'S'Wonderful' and the 'Fate' motif of Beethoven's 5th. The intellectual pretensions of the heroine are satirized, of course, the musical film always preferring energy over reason, entertainment over art. Yet this is balanced by the film's equally comic observation of brash American commercialism ('Think Pink!') and of innocent Americans abroad. 'Here it comes,' chant the Parisian chauffeurs, 'the great American tourist!'

If Astaire seems somewhat old for Hepburn as a romantic partner, one should remember that Miss Hepburn made something of a speciality of enchanting Hollywood's eminent senior citizens on film (Humphrey Bogart, Henry Fonda, Gary Cooper, Cary Grant and Rex Harrison were only some of her screen lovers). Also, when Astaire steps out, the years seem to disappear. He does extraordinary things with hat, umbrella and raincoat in his 'Let's kiss and make up' routine, his temporary tiff with the heroine expanded choreographically into a comic bullfight. Needless to say, both draw in their horns, and Paris exerts its spell. As a response to the film, one can only echo the words of the song with which the two lovers are finally reunited: 'S'Wonderful . . . S'Marvellous . . .'

LEFT: Audrey Hepburn models a red dress at the Louvre. She is later to say of the fashion world: 'It feels wonderful, but it's not me.'
FAR LEFT: 'How long has this been going on?' Bookshop assistant Jo (Audrey Hepburn) ruminates about the first stirrings of romantic love.
RIGHT: 'Think Pink'. Magazine editor Maggie Prescott (Kay Thompson) sets the fashions for the coming year.
BELOW: Balloons in Paris. Fashion photographer Dick Avery (Fred Astaire, in raincoat) gives final instructions to his young protegée (Audrey Hepburn), with whom he is falling in love.

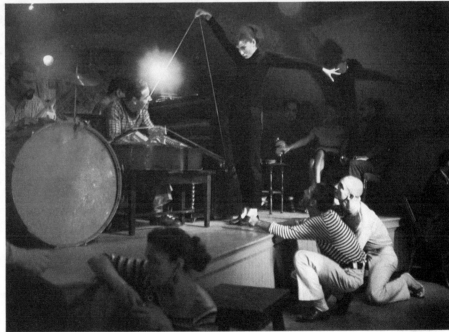

OPPOSITE: 'Clap Yo Hands!' Kay Thompson and a bearded Astaire (on floor, with guitar) let rip.
TOP: The Great American Tourists. Kay Thompson, Fred Astaire and Audrey Hepburn encounter each other at the Eiffel Tower and together bid 'Bonjour' to Paris. A typical musical celebration of a big city.

ABOVE: 'Basal Metabolism'. Audrey Hepburn dances a suitably sultry number in the Left Bank night club where she meets her existentialist philosopher-hero (Michel Auclair). Astaire has warned her about him: 'He's about as interested in your intellect as I am!'

BELOW: Maria (Julie Andrews) leaves the convent to take on her job as governess, with only her guitar and her 'confidence' to help her. Note the bars of the convent behind her: they will be recalled when she approaches the Captain's house, two different kinds of prison which she will liberate.
RIGHT: Captain von Trapp (Christopher Plummer) summons the children to order with his ship's whistle, to Maria's astonished horror.
FAR RIGHT: Beauty falls in love with the Beast. Maria transforms the household and the heart of the Captain. Here they declare their love.
BOTTOM: Maria meets the children.
RIGHT: The von Trapp family escape across the mountains to safety.

THE SOUND OF MUSIC

USA 1965
DIRECTED BY ROBERT WISE

Producer: *Robert Wise*
Screenplay: *Ernest Lehman*
Based on the stage musical by
Richard Rodgers and
Oscar Hammerstein and book by
Howard Lindsay and Russel Crouse
Music supervised and directed by
Irwin Kostal
Photography: *Ted McCord*
20th-Century Fox. 172 mins

Leading players:
*Julie Andrews,
Christopher Plummer,
Eleanor Parker, Richard Haydn,
Peggy Wood.*

Nobody likes *The Sound of Music* – except the general public. The critical intelligentsia has scoffed at what it sees as a schmaltzy melange of music and mountains, nuns and Nazis. But from the opening helicopter shot, which immediately exploits the scenic grandeur and visually anticipates the soaring spirit of the heroine, the film seems to have absolute certainty in its wide-ranging sentimental appeal. Its confidence is not misplaced: it is still the most successful film musical ever made.

A lot of clever calculation has gone into this commercial confection. The situation is really that of Beauty (a convent girl, Maria, played with crisp authority by Julie Andrews) stealing the heart of the Beast (Christopher Plummer at his most sarcastically saturnine as Captain von Trapp) from under the nose of the wicked fairy (the thankless role of the Baroness played with great dignity by Eleanor Parker). But the story is true: convent-girl Maria really did marry her Captain and escape from the Nazis with him and the children across the

Austrian Alps. Because the story itself seems such a delicious mixture of fairy-tale and fact, it provides the ideal vehicle for a musical which, like most musicals, is dedicated to the proposition that dreams can come true.

The film is also interesting in its insights into the role of women. The plot is *Jane Eyre* set to music. A governess with an independent spirit falls in love with her stern master whose forbidding façade is melted by her humane example. After the removal of various impediments, viewer, she married him. In the process, she liberalizes the Captain's stuffy views on class and women. She breaks down the prison of his restricted attitudes (significantly, the gates of the house when she first arrives recall the gates of the enclosed order of the convent). She demolishes the foolish tyranny of his domestic rule (the whistle whereby he earlier summoned his children is intriguingly recalled towards the end when that boy whistles for his Nazi colleagues). What Maria does is to effect the transformation of a totalitarian house-

hold into a democratic family. She succeeds in this whilst retaining her femininity, freedom and identity. Subliminally, this may be the reason that women seem to love the film so much.

All of this is achieved through the talisman of music. Music expresses Maria's love of nature ('The Sound of Music') and gives her confidence. It vitalizes the children ('Do-Re-Mi') and banishes their fears ('My Favourite Things'). It transforms the Captain when he hears music in his house again, and the moment when he first sings is the moment, one feels, when Maria falls in love (there is some beautiful filming here). Music finally encapsulates a national spirit and celebrates a disappearing world ('Edelweiss'). Whatever critics might say, no survey of the musical could omit *The Sound of Music*, for it is actually about music – the wide varieties of emotion music can express and what, ultimately, the sound of music can *do*.

FANTASY AND IMAGINATION

Metropolis (1926) · *Fantasia* (1940) · *Orphée* (1950) ·
2001: A Space Odyssey (1968) ·
Close Encounters of the Third Kind (1977)

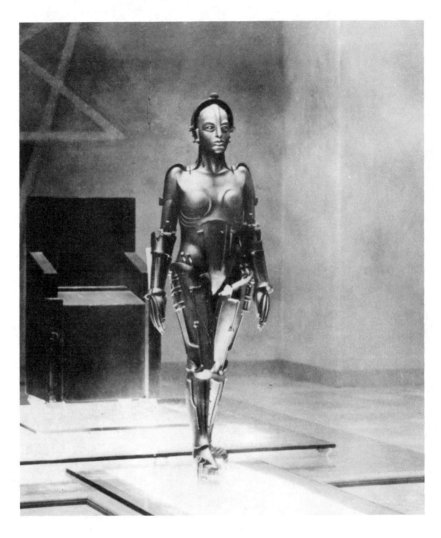

The cinema has created many fantastic new worlds, exploring the threat and yet the fascination of the unknown.
ABOVE: The robot in *Metropolis*.
LEFT: Waiting for the starship to land in *Close Encounters of the Third Kind*.

ABOVE LEFT: An example of the incredible, geometrically patterned sets of *Metropolis*. The tycoon Frederson (Alfred Abel) paces his office. LEFT: The appearance of the true Maria (Brigitte Helm), her saint-like innocence symbolized by the surrounding children who put their trust in her. BOTTOM: The false, robot Maria incites revolt amongst the workers. In contrast to the picture above, Maria is seen leading a mob of frenzied adults. TOP RIGHT: One of the film's most famous images, expressing the mechanized dehumanization of the working-class under the tyranny of their employers. The worker here is in fact the tycoon's son, Freder (Gustav Fröhlich), who, inspired by Maria, is discovering what killing labour supports the city. FAR RIGHT: During the workers' revolt, the monster-machines are destroyed. BOTTOM RIGHT: Amidst the wreckage of the city, the false Maria is burned, witch-like, at the stake, by the mob who were eager to follow her but have now rejected her.

METROPOLIS

GERMANY 1926
DIRECTED BY FRITZ LANG

Screenplay: *Fritz Lang and Thea von Harbou*
Based on the novel by
Thea von Harbou
Photography: *Karl Freund and Gunther Rittau*
Special effects:
Eugen Schufftan
UFA. 104 mins

Leading players:
Brigitte Helm, Alfred Abel, Gustav Fröhlich, Rudolf Klein-Rogge.

'Man is seized by his own creation, The City, and is made into its creature, its extensive organ and finally its victim,' wrote the philosopher Oswald Spengler in his book, *The Decline of the West* (1918). Fritz Lang's film, *Metropolis*, is a continuation of this idea, a nightmare fantasy inspired by Lang's first sight of the skyscrapers of New York, and a mammoth film enterprise that required a cast of over thirty thousand and a shooting schedule of over three hundred days.

The basic idea of *Metropolis* is its concept of the modern world as a symbolically constructed city. Lang presents three interlocking images: the City as Prison, a Kafkaesque construction in which existence is conceived as a series of inescapable traps; the City as Moloch, a creature that destroys and devours its children; and the City as Tower of Babel, in which the workers are alienated from the creation that is dependent on their labour and in which the people who have the vision do not do the work.

The different strata of the Metropolis reflect the social order. The rulers live in skyscrapers and the workers toil beneath the earth, seething with unrest. When the city's ruler discovers that his son is not only sympathetic to the disgruntled workers but enamoured of an employee, Maria, he consults a mad scientist, Rotwang. Together they construct a false Maria, a robot, to engineer a revolt which will give the ruler an excuse to crush the workers. The revolt occurs and violence ensues, but a compromise is reached when the ruler discovers that his son has not been killed, as he feared.

Ostensibly, the atmosphere of persecution might seem diffiult to reconcile with the compassionate conclusion. It is the fevered imagery one remembers, the picture of a world dehumanized and distorted through exploitation. Lang himself subsequently thought the ending of *Metropolis* rather facile, with its advocacy of a human harmony between Capital and Labour (though he was pleased with his forecast for the future – 'In 1924 I am already prophesying overhead motorways'). But the ending might be more ambiguous than it appears. Has the son really converted the father or has the father outwitted the son, professing a humanity which will enable him to capture the workers' hearts and thus exert a more complete and subtle domination over them?

Metropolis was apparently a favourite film of Adolf Hitler's, who saw the ending as signifying that responsible rule is a matter of the heart as well as the head. His approval sits ironically on a film whose creation of the wicked city and the madmen who run it has been interpreted as prophetic of the coming of Nazism. (Lang was to flee Germany to America on Hitler's accession to power.) *Metropolis* might not be Lang's most likeable or coherent film, but it is certainly his most ambitious and influential. For the roots of, for example, Kubrick's *Dr Strangelove* (1964). Godard's *Alphaville* (1965), not to mention countless science-fiction screen extravaganzas, one need look no further than to *Metropolis*.

FANTASIA

USA 1940
DIRECTED BY WALT DISNEY

PRODUCTION SUPERVISOR:
Ben Sharpsteen
Story direction:
Joe Grant and Dick Huemer
Music: BACH: *Toccata and
Fugue in D Minor;*
TCHAIKOVSKY: *The Nutcracker
Suite;* DUKAS: *The Sorcerer's
Apprentice;* STRAVINSKY: *The
Rite of Spring;* BEETHOVEN:
Pastoral Symphony;
PONCHIELLI: *Dance of the Hours;*
MUSSORGSKY: *Night on Bare
Mountain;* SCHUBERT: *Ave Maria.*
The Philadelphia Orchestra,
conducted by *Leopold Stokowski*
Disney Production/RKO release.
135 mins.

Just as the French directors of the *nouvelle
vague* claimed to have discovered
Shakespeare through Orson Welles, many
people could well have discovered classi-
cal music through *Fantasia.* Some might
not have forgiven Walt Disney for that. As
Leonard Bernstein instructed a 1973 Har-
vard audience: 'Try to think of Beethoven's
Pastoral Symphony without Disney
nymphs and centaurs.'

The idea for the film is said to have
come from Disney's desire to cast Mickey
Mouse as the Sorcerer's Apprentice, the
mouse's prancings to Dukas's music being
ultimately one of the highlights of the
film. From that, and from Disney's
continual experimentation with the fusion
of sight and sound and the possibility of
stereophony, the idea developed of a
feature-length attempt to illustrate some of
the world's great music. It would be a kind
of children's concert, designed to bring a
mass audience to the classics and, more
subtly, to bring a highbrow audience to
Disney. Outraging musical purists, who
resented the simplistic pictorialization of
sophisticated musical argument, *Fantasia*
became one of Disney's most controversial
films, as well as the film which perhaps
best illustrates the diversity of Disney's
ambitions and appeal – as entertainer,
educator and innovator.

The film is full of that humour,
sentiment and innocence that is the
hallmark of the cinema's most popular and
dependable provider of family entertainment. Comic mushrooms mince around
to the strains of Tchaikovsky, whilst, in the
mock-ballet of 'Dance of the Hours',
hippos flop with absurd gentility and aerial
views of choreographic patterns provide a
delicious animated parody of Busby Berkeley. For uplifting sentiment, the film
concludes with a fulsome visual and aural
rendering of *Ave Maria.*

However, *Fantasia* is not a film which
plays safe, or subsumes everything into
commercial cuteness. Bach's *Toccata and
Fugue in D Minor* is matched to abstract
patterns of lines and shapes to reflect the
strict form of the music. Stravinsky's *Rite
of Spring* (a bold choice for inclusion) is
visually interpreted as an expression of the
evolution of the world, with the music's
barbaric rhythms effectively matched to

images of dinosaurs and primitive struggle. Beethoven might have suffered most,
the symphony being reduced to about
twenty minutes, but there is a real lilt in
Stokowski's performance, and charm and
imagination pervade the screen from the
storm onwards.

It is probably true that, although the
music generates the images, it ultimately
becomes subordinate to them. Attempting
to popularize famous music, *Fantasia*
might finally have had equal success in
enlarging the expressiveness of the cartoon
film. In either event, the experiment of
Uncle Walt was vindicated. Not immediately. The film initially failed, a fact
on which a critic of the time commented
smugly: 'It proves for once that crime does
not pay.' But its subsequent revivals
proved very successful. On its reissue in
1946, a jingle for the film claimed:
'*Fantasia* will amaze ya.' For succeeding
generations, it still does.

FAR LEFT: Mickey Mouse as the Sorcerer's Apprentice. Disney's desire to cast Mickey as the Apprentice generated the idea for the whole film.

TOP LEFT: The unlikely but effective mincing mushrooms, dancing to the rhythm of Tchaikovsky's *Nutcracker Suite*. An example of the film's sometimes comic choreography.

MIDDLE LEFT: A larky crocodile makes an appearance during Ponchielli's *Dance of the Hours*. He is delighted to find a hippo for his *pas de deux*.

BOTTOM LEFT: In contrast to Disney's famed cuteness, a chilling demon appears in the vivid horror-animation of Mussorgsky's *Night on Bare Mountain*.

TOP: Disney ingeniously interpreted Stravinsky's *Rite of Spring* in terms of the evolution of the world and primeval struggle. Stravinsky's barbaric rhythms effectively accompany the dinosaurs on their rampage.

ABOVE: One of the more controversial settings in the film. Beethoven's Pastoral Symphony (No. 6 in F.) is illustrated by excessively coy imagery, of which these flying horses are a good example.

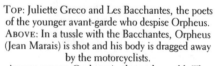

TOP: Juliette Greco and Les Bacchantes, the poets of the younger avant-garde who despise Orpheus.
ABOVE: In a tussle with the Bacchantes, Orpheus (Jean Marais) is shot and his body is dragged away by the motorcyclists.
ABOVE RIGHT: Orpheus in the underworld. The Princess (Maria Casarès), the young poet Cegeste (Edouard Dermithe, kneeling), who has been revived by the Princess, the chauffeur Heurtebise (François Perier), and Orpheus.
RIGHT: Orpheus and Heurtebise proceed along the perilous corridor of the underworld, watched by an old woman, played by Jean Cocteau himself.
FAR RIGHT: Heurtebise appears as a witness at an underworld tribunal. The Princess is on trial for having killed Eurydice (Maria Déa, right), without orders.
BOTTOM RIGHT: The final scene. Heurtebise and the Princess, guilty of disobeying their superiors, are marched off to face a terrible punishment.

ORPHÉE

FRANCE 1950
DIRECTED BY JEAN COCTEAU

Producer: *Emile Darbon*
Screenplay: *Jean Cocteau*
Music: *Georges Auric*
Photography: *Nicholas Hayer*
95 mins

Leading players:
*Jean Marais, François Perier,
Maria Casarès, Marie Déa,
Edouard Dermithe, Juliette Greco.*

'I was convinced that in the case of an unusual and difficult film, the curiosity that brings people to see it is stronger than the laziness that keeps them away.' So said Jean Cocteau of *Orphée*. Cocteau believed that art should astound and astonish, and that the cinema was a place of magic which enabled the artist to hypnotize an audience into dreaming the same dream. An artist whose only ambition was to please and convince, thought Cocteau, was like a flower whose only ambition was to end up in a vase.

Orphée is a magical film. It re-tells the Orpheus legend but sets it in modern Paris. Orpheus (Jean Marais) is an eminent poet, loved by the public but despised by fellow-poets of the younger and more experimental school. Happily married to Eurydice (Marie Déa), Orpheus nevertheless becomes fascinated by a black-clad patroness of the arts, the Princess (Maria Casarès, whose eyes seem compelling enough to pierce the dark), who is accompanied by a chauffeur and flanked by motorcyclists in dark glasses. Gradually it is revealed that the Princess is the Angel of Death; the chauffeur is her Charon, boatman to the underworld; and the motorcyclists the messengers of Death. When Death seems to have claimed Eurydice, Orpheus journeys into the underworld to reclaim his wife but also to meet the Princess again, with whom he has become infatuated.

The film operates on many levels. As a tale of mystery and suspense, it is grippingly sustained. The menacing, goggled figures on motorcycles have now become a screen convention, cropping up with variations in films like *Psycho* and *Don*

Siegel's *The Killers* (1964) as harbingers of Death. The film is also compelling simply as a sequence of stunning images, notably when a mirror ripples and then dissolves so that Death can pass through into her kingdom, and when Orpheus journeys to the Underworld past ruined buildings, following Heurtebise/Charon in a range of speed and movement that recalls moments from everyone's dreams. To some degree, it is also a self-portrait in which Cocteau who, like Orpheus, feels he is esteemed by the public but despised by the avant-garde, wrestles with the problem of creation, and with the conflict between finding inspiration in the real world or risking oblivion by searching into the deepest recesses of the imagination, the underworld of the human personality.

The Orpheus/Cocteau artist is somewhat similar to the artist figure in *Death in Venice*: aloof, arrogant, suddenly possessed by a vision of Beauty which might be Death itself, but having an artist's curiosity to pursue this mystery to its conclusion, which might actually lie beyond the grave. It is a film which explores the proximity of Life and Death, Reality and Illusion. It shows Cocteau's total commitment to the world of his own artistry, which seems to have its own logic and obey its own laws. 'It is not necessary to understand,' says the chauffeur to Orpheus, 'it is necessary only to believe.' Cocteau's 'unreal' world becomes persuasive through the very intensity of its realization.

2001: A SPACE ODYSSEY

GB 1968
DIRECTED BY STANLEY KUBRICK

Producer: *Stanley Kubrick*
Screenplay: *Stanley Kubrick and Arthur C. Clarke*
Based on the story *The Sentinel* by Arthur C. Clarke
Music: *Richard Strauss, Johann Strauss, Aram Khachaturian, Gyorgy Ligeti*
Photography: *Geoffrey Unsworth*
MGM. 141 mins

Leading players:
Keir Dullea, Gary Lockwood, William Sylvester.

2001: A Space Odyssey is a step into a brave new world. No epic since *Intolerance* had been so completely the vision of one man. Stanley Kubrick's odyssey has no hero and little plot, but communicates as an overwhelming visual and musical experience.

The film could be described as a fantastic symphony in three movements. The first is 'The Dawn of Man', in which primordial apes fight for survival and discover a seemingly natural inclination towards aggression. A bone becomes a weapon of destruction, then is tossed into the air, and, in the most remarkable matching cut in screen history, is visually displaced by a shot of a spinning spacecraft. In one shot, there has been an astonishing leap in time and technology, but the matching cut implies that the same leap might not have been made between the behaviour of apes and men. The film's second part deals with a space mission to investigate a mysterious signal emanating from Jupiter, a mission jeopardized when the speaking computer HAL tries to eliminate the crew. The final part is a journey beyond Jupiter, which opens up an infinite sense of space whilst also confronting man with a contemplation of himself and his past, which will surely influence the path he takes in the future.

All three parts are linked by the appearance at various stages of a mysterious rectangular monolith. This monolith seems to represent a higher intelligence, the next stage of development, power and knowledge towards which man is always reaching. The film is about man's constant quest after new intelligence, as he takes what Kubrick calls 'the next step of his evolutionary destiny'.

The film's futuristic observation is often humorous, like that deadpan shot of the air hostess as she calmly turns upside down whilst delivering the processed meals, or the zero gravity toilet with its bewildering multitude of instructions, or even the small-screen appearance of a greying Kenneth Kendall to read the news on BBC 12. As befits a space fantasia, music is very important. Johann Strauss's *Blue Danube* waltz rhythmically enfolds shots of the floating spacecraft, a ballet of machinery, an ingenious modern concept of the music of the spheres. Richard Strauss's musical tone poem of Nietzsche's *Also Sprach Zarathustra* accompanies the 'Dawn of Man' section, an appropriate reference for a film concerned with man's fitness for survival and evolution and his super-human attempts to master the universe.

The film is a speculation more than a thesis. It is not without disturbing implications. Women have little function in this world, it seems, and, more generally, one is struck by the absence of human feeling. Communication is perfunctory, banal, and more often dependent on computer data than human interplay, and individual identity is subsumed under a robotic quiet efficiency. HAL is the only sympathetic creature, a crazed computer who runs amok and takes revenge on his creators. Has man been mastered by the technology he himself has constructed? Perhaps the very greatness of 2001 suggests not. Among other things, it demonstrates how man's increasing technical accomplishment can enhance the expressiveness of the most technological of art forms, the cinema.

PREVIOUS PAGE: The spacecraft from the third part of Stanley Kubrick's film. The journey to Jupiter across the Solar System. *Inset:* The interior of the spacecraft.
BELOW: Kubrick's wide-screen vision of the moon's surface. The second part of the film deals with a mission to the moon, investigating mysterious signals being transmitted by a black monolith.
RIGHT: The astronaut Bowman (Keir Dullea) fights his way back into the spacecraft through an airlock to disconnect the computer, HAL, which has run amok and caused the death of his comrade, Poole (Gary Lockwood).
CENTRE: An eye image from the final stage of the austronaut's journey to the beyond, one of the numerous circular images in the film used to underline the theme of man's cyclical development.
BOTTOM: Bowman contemplates himself and his past, dying in order to be reborn. 'If the film stirs the emotions and penetrates the subconscious,' said Kubrick, 'if it stimulates the viewer's mythological and religious yearnings, then it has succeeded.'

CLOSE ENCOUNTERS OF THE THIRD KIND

USA 1977
DIRECTED BY STEVEN SPIELBERG

Producers: *Julia Phillips and Michael Phillips*
Screenplay: *Steven Spielberg*
Music: *John Williams*
Photography: *Vilmos Zsigmond*
Special photographic effects: *Douglas Trumbull*
Columbia. 135 mins

Leading players:
*Richard Dreyfuss,
François Truffaut, Teri Garr,
Melinda Dillon, Cary Guffey.*

In sharp contrast to the Cold War strategies of 1950s science-fiction cinema and unlike the cool intellectual vision of Kubrick's *2001*, *Close Encounters of the Third Kind* asserts the wonder rather than the terror of the unknown. Richard Dreyfuss plays a suburban electrician hypnotically drawn into contact with unidentified friendly objects. The progress of events by which he comes not only to observe but be accepted as a passenger on the alien spacecraft is offered not as a cautionary tale but an uplifting spectacle.

If Kubrick's sci-fi extravaganza aims to make you think, Spielberg's is designed to make you feel. There is a fresh, innocent directness about his approach to films. His cinema communicates in the way that communication is established with the UFOs in this film: not through language and complex messages, but through a transmission of visual signs supported by music.

If Spielberg is not a thinker, he does have an uncanny sense of how to work on an audience. His heroes are ordinary people whose lives suddenly become adventures: it is analogous to the oldest impulse of cinema-going as a means of escape from reality into fantasy. He invariably contrives it so that the hero succeeds in overcoming his fears or inhibitions, but these triumphs are presented with wit rather than solemnity. In *Close Encounters*, Dreyfuss's transformation is so sympathetic because the humour increases his humanity. When a UFO first appears behind his car, he is so unperceptive that he waves it on – as funny and well-timed a moment as the first appearance of the shark behind Roy Scheider in *Jaws*. His gathering obsession is estab-

lished very often in comic detail, like that moment where, watched by his bewildered family, he abstractedly works his mashed potato into the shape of the mountain that is haunting him.

Later, Spielberg was to re-issue a special edition of *Close Encounters*, with the mid-section tightened, and the finale somewhat extended. But if one has not been overwhelmed by the technology to begin with, it is doubtful whether these narrative adjustments would make much difference. The aim is to provide a collective visual experience which induces in an audience an almost religious sense of awe. It is not accidental that Dreyfuss is

glimpsed watching *The Ten Commandments* on television. If *Jaws* showed Spielberg very effectively adopting the suspense mechanisms of Hitchock, *Close Encounters* shows him as he dons the epic mantle of a Cecil B. DeMille. The awesome landing of the spacecraft is Spielberg's parting of the Red Sea, his technical miracle, his reaffirmation of the cinema as a place of magic. The ending has additional significance. One extra-terrestrial might get it into his head to stick around on earth: there is the seed here of *E.T.* Also the hero's disappearance into space might be prophetic of Spielberg himself: his horizons seem limitless.

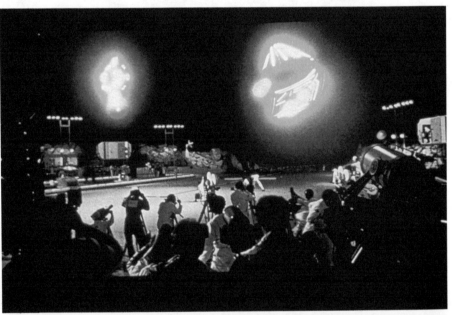

Opposite, top: The research of a team of scientists has led them to mystical India. They hear the mysterious chant which seems to prophesy the coming of the extra-terrestrials.
Left: Richard Dreyfuss (right) fashions an outline of the shape which is obsessing him, watched and encouraged by Melinda Dillon and her son Cary Guffey, who have also come into contact with the UFOs. The mountain-like shape is the key to the location where the aliens will land.
Above left: Richard Dreyfuss plays the baffled hero, almost overwhelmed by his extraordinary experiences but swept along by the adventure.
Top right: The team of scientists watch the spectacular light show as the smaller UFOs prepare the way for the landing of the mother ship.
Right: The film's most awesome special effect, the star ship coming into view and preparing to land.

HORROR

Nosferatu (1922) · *Frankenstein* (1931) · *King Kong* (1933) · *Psycho* (1960)

The horror film has often been used to debate serious and relevant themes, such as the aspirations of man, and the unthinking cruelty of scientists who become detached from human feelings. Thus the monster has sometimes emerged as a more sympathetic figure than the humans.

ABOVE: Boris Karloff's melancholy monster, the creation of a scientist, in *Frankenstein*.

LEFT: Kong, subdued and humiliated, on display in a New York theatre in *King Kong*. His captors hope for huge profits.

NOSFERATU

GERMANY 1922
DIRECTED BY F. W. MURNAU

Screenplay: *Henrik Galeen*
Based on the novel *Dracula*,
by Bram Stoker
Photography: *Fritz Arno Wagner*
62 mins

Leading players:
Max Schreck,
Gustav von Wagenheim,
Greta Schroder.

F. W. Murnau's *Nosferatu* was the screen's first treatment of the *Dracula* story. It contains all the elements that have since become so familiar, like the monster's sleep in the coffin by day and his drinking of blood by night, and the destruction of the monster through the sacrifice of a pure woman who will stay by his side until after cock-crow. 'Nosferatu' is a Rumanian word meaning 'undead',

and the story is that of a young clerk, Jonathan Harker, who discovers Nosferatu's evil whilst visiting him in his castle to complete the sale of a house. Imprisoned in the castle, Harker has to escape to warn his wife and the villagers of the approaching danger.

With sharp claws, fangs and even sharp ears, Max Schreck's Nosferatu is an unmistakable embodiment of evil, which will emphasize the nobility of Nina Harker's supreme sacrifice. Nosferatu has heard Nina's warning cry to Jonathan (her love and fear creating a telepathy between her and her husband) and journeys towards her on a phantom ship, infecting and killing the crew with his evil. The sinister shot of the contaminated ship as it sails into Bremen harbour, the sight of the city gripped by mysterious plague, the monstrously distorted shadows as Nosferatu comes to claim Nina, constitute some of the most chilling images of the horror film.

Unlike many similar German films of the period, much of Nosferatu was shot on location, a rare example of visual distortion being the use of negative images as Harker is driven by coach to Nosferatu's castle. Elsewhere the impression of nature in uproar is conveyed by Murnau's ability to invest the real world with an eerie atmosphere, through the depiction of nervous animal life, bleak landscape and misty woodlands, out of which the castle emerges menacingly at the pinnacle of a cliff. Like many great fantasies, Nosferatu has a basic realism; its world has a sinister solidity. There is the suggestion that Nosferatu is not simply a monster on a literal level, but symbolically represents the potential monstrousness in Harker – more generally, in the heart of all men – that must be repressed. The rats which accompany Nosferatu are not simply a traditional horror device but symbolize an invasion of evil and an infection of fear. Interestingly, similar rodent symbolism is to occur in two of the great political novels of the century, George Orwell's 1984 and Albert Camus's *The Plague*, and it has become quite customary to interpret *Nosferatu* politically as a prophecy of the coming of Nazism (like the preceding *Cabinet of Dr Caligari* and the subsequent *Metropolis*). Perhaps this is being wise after the event and pinning the film too closely to one specific meaning. *Nosferatu* is about evil unleashed on a complacent community, and the terrible sacrifice that has to be made in order to check the spread of such infection. The theme might be couched in supernatural terms, but it is relevant to the world in which we live.

FAR LEFT: Nosferatu (Max Schreck) stands in the archway, with claws at the ready, just before Nina sees him.
CENTRE: Nosferatu with his visitor, Jonathan Harker (Gustav von Wangenheim) who seems pardonably alarmed at the appearance of his host. 'You are late, young man,' says Nosferatu. 'It is almost midnight.'
ABOVE: During the journey to Bremen aboard the *Demeter*, Nosferatu appears ominously from below, edging towards the Captain, who has tied himself to the wheel.
TOP: Nosferatu emerges from the hold where he has been travelling in his coffin full of earth. The sailors are now all dead, the hold is alive with rats, and Nosferatu's evil is about to be unleashed on the community. 'The most important film every made in Germany,' said the modern German director, Werner Herzog, of *Nosferatu*. He was to remake the film in 1979.

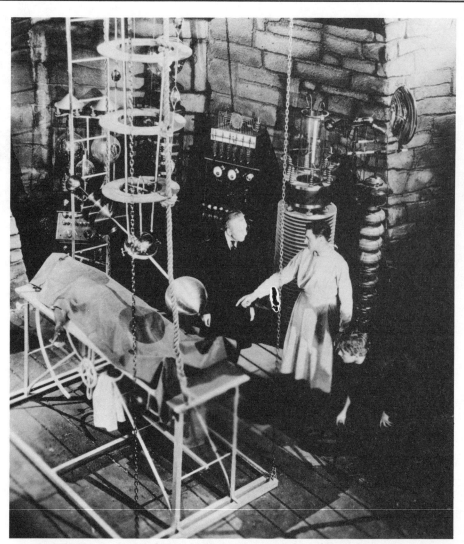

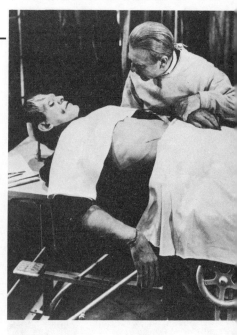

LEFT: Dr Frankenstein (Colin Clive) in his laboratory, with his assistants (Edward Van Sloan, left, and Dwight Frye, right).
ABOVE: Edward Van Sloan examines the monster (Boris Karloff) on the slab.
BELOW: The monster is subdued by fire, one of the incidents which dramatizes his oppression and builds up an audience's sympathy.
RIGHT: The scene by the lake, showing the monster's gentle curiosity, and the girl's fearless innocence. His distorted frame contrasts with the natural beauty of the setting. He has been given a flower by the girl. Her action precedes his inadvertent murder of her.
FAR RIGHT: The final scene at the windmill, where the enraged monster is cornered by an unruly mob. The climax confirms the monster as more a victim than a villain, turned into an outcast by the reactions of so-called normal society.

FRANKENSTEIN

USA 1931
DIRECTED BY JAMES WHALE

Producer: *Carl Laemmle Jr*
Screenplay: *Garret Fort,*
Francis Edward Faragoh,
John L. Balderston
Based on the play by Peggy Webling
and the novel by
Mary Wollstonecraft Shelley
Photography: *Arthur Edeson*
Universal. 71 mins

Leading players:
Boris Karloff, Colin Clive,
Mae Clark, John Boles,
Edward Van Sloan, Dwight Frye.

The instant success of *Frankenstein* led to the inevitable sequels: *The Bride of Frankenstein* (1935), *Son of Frankenstein* (1939), *Frankenstein Meets the Wolf Man* (1943) etc. The interesting thing about these titles is their perpetuation of the common confusion whereby Frankenstein is assumed to be the name of the Monster (in fact, he has no name) and not,

as is the case, the name of the scientist who created him. Inadvertently, this confusion reinforces a major theme of the original: who is the real monster of the story?

The story of *Frankenstein* has always had great appeal. It can be taken as an indictment of scientific irresponsibility, in which science gives birth to a creation it cannot control – a particularly topical theme of our century. Connected with that is a religious sub-theme in which scientific ambition is seen as a form of desecration. Science attempts to usurp the laws of the Universe by controlling life and death, and the birth of the creature thus becomes a blasphemous resurrection.

The story's main feature is its sympathy for the Monster. He is not demonic but oppressed. In the film, he is treated as a backward butler. Because of the Monster's proletarian clothes and Colin Clive's appropriately pompous performance as the scientist, the relationship between Frankenstein and the Monster has an undercurrent of social protest. The film's sense of class outrage might derive from director James Whale's own modest background in England, and might partially explain the film's contemporary popularity with the Depression-stricken, predominantly working-class audience. The Monster's life has been distorted and will be destroyed by forces beyond his control.

It is hard to remember that the part of the Monster was originally assigned to Bella Lugosi. Boris Karlof makes the part his own. He never speaks – it is one of the great silent film performances. Aided by the remarkable make-up of Universal's Jack Pierce, who conceived the Monster's elongated arms and distorted head, Karloff attains eloquence through grunts, gait and gesture. He delights in sunlight and nature, and his face radiates happiness when taking the gift of flowers from the girl by the lake. His murder of the girl is an act of ignorance, not malevolence: in throwing her into the lake, he is expecting her to float like a flower.

Particularly commendable in the film are its understated violence, which is imaginatively implied rather than graphically shown; its restrained use of music; and its impish black humour (like the shot of the cheerfully bobbing skeleton in the laboratory, or of that bottle so obligingly labelled: 'Abnormal Brain'). Evidence of its continuing power to enthral is provided in the highly praised Spanish film, *Spirit of the Beehive* (1973), which interestingly explores the impact of *Frankenstein* on a number of children when they see it at their local mobile cinema. Their response – an absence of adult prejudice that makes them more fascinated than afraid – seems to take us back to that scene by the lake, where the little girl perceived the gentle soul behind the fearful frame. By the end of *Frankenstein*, the man-made Monster has something of the air of the Noble Savage. His fate exemplifies the monstrousness of Man.

ABOVE: The film crew arrives on Skull Island and confronts the hostile islanders. 'Steady with those rifles, boys,' says the director Denham (Robert Armstrong, centre), when they are discovered spying on a secret native ceremony.
RIGHT: After they have kidnapped Ann and offered her as a sacrifice to Kong, the natives gather along the top of the Great Wall chanting an invocation to him.
FAR RIGHT: Ann (Fay Wray) looks on in horror as Kong defends her from a pterodactyl.
BOTTOM RIGHT: The finale on the Empire State Building. After being attacked by swooping biplanes, Kong has realized the end is near and has put Ann down on a ledge to be rescued. 'Oh no, it wasn't the airplanes . . . it was Beauty killed the Beast,' says Denham. Like Frankenstein's monster, Kong is another beast moved by love and beauty, a Quasimodo of the jungle.

KING KONG

USA 1933

DIRECTED BY
MERIAN C. COOPER AND
ERNEST B. SCHOEDSACK

Producers: *Merian C. Cooper and Ernest B. Schoedsack*
Executive producer: *David O. Selznick*
Screenplay: *James A. Creelman and Ruth Rose*
Based on an idea by Merian C. Cooper and Edgar Wallace
Special effects: *Willis H. O'Brien*
Music: *Max Steiner*
Photography: *Eddie Linden, Vernon Walker, J. O. Taylor*
RKO. 100 mins

Leading players:
Fay Wray, Robert Armstrong, Bruce Cabot.

'No money, yet New York dug up $89,931 in four days to see *King Kong*,' screamed a headline of the trade paper *Variety* in 1933. The headline highlights the enormous immediate success of *King Kong*. Inadvertently, it might also hint at one reason for that success. At the height of the Depression ('No Money!'), might not audiences have enjoyed the sight of a giant ape raging at and ripping out the guts of America's financial headquarters?

It would not do to push too far the notion of *King Kong* as Karl Marx in a gorilla suit, proclaiming the end of Capitalism from his vantage point at the top of the Empire State Building. Basically, the film is intended as a finely fashioned fantasy about a misunderstood monster in a modern metropolis. Kong has been brought to New York after being discovered on Skull Island by an intrepid film crew, who have trapped him by exploiting the monster's crush on the crew's leading lady Ann (Fay Wray). Kong's love for Ann

has turned him into a Quasimodo of the jungle, protecting his lady from a variety of perils that include an omnivorous dinosaur, a pterodactyl and a giant snake. On the whole, Kong would seem a better romantic prospect for Ann than the ship's first mate, Driscoll (Bruce Cabot).

Cooper, Schoedsack and Willis O'Brien had previously devised elaborate adventure sequences in their works, notably in O'Brien's 1931 film, *Creation*, and in the Cooper–Schoedsack collaboration of 1932, *The Most Dangerous Game*, known as *The Hounds of Zaroff* in England. But *King Kong* represents the culmination of their efforts. Undoubtedly the film's greatest achievement, though, is not so much in the action as in the characterization of Kong. Max Steiner's ambitious musical portraiture underlines his tenderness and emotional feeling, and Willis O'Brien's brilliant model and animation work humanizes the creature's curiosity and love of beauty. O'Brien's

pupil, Ray Harryhausen rightly said: 'O'Brien injected into a pile of rubber and metal joints far more sympathy and depth than was to be found in the real people on the screen.' It is for this reason that the film's last line – 'It wasn't the airplanes, it was *Beauty* killed the Beast' – seems valid and moving.

Kong's raging destruction in the last part of the film is terrifying but understandable and even justifiable, given his uprooting from his natural habitat and his being put so ignominiously on show to the public for crude commercial profit. The adventure is the thing, of course, but Kong as a victim, protesting against the commercial chains of modern society, should not be entirely overlooked. Perhaps Fay Wray (whose skilfully sustained hysteria is one of the film's enduring highlights) was indirectly alluding to this social sub-theme in an interview in 1973 when she said: 'If we'd had a percentage deal, we wouldn't be such nice people. We'd be rich.'

PSYCHO

USA 1960

DIRECTED BY
ALFRED HITCHCOCK

Producer: *Alfred Hitchcock*
Screenplay: *Joseph Stefano*
Based on the novel by Robert Bloch
Music: *Bernard Herrmann*
Photography: *John L. Russell*
Paramount. 108 mins

Leading players:
Anthony Perkins, Janet Leigh,
Vera Miles, John Gavin,
Martin Balsam.

Was Alfred Hitchcock what he seemed? His public persona was that of a portly gentleman with a macabre sense of humour who, as a film-maker, spices the civilities of our lives with a touch of healthy melodrama. From a different angle, however, his films look like the dreams in the dark of a very complicated man. The suspense derives mostly from sexual anxiety, and the films disclose a perverse personality who punishes his heroines for their beauty and whose perception of the commingling of love and hate, fear and desire reveals the obsessions of a Freudian psychologist.

Psycho brilliantly demonstrates this split in Hitchcock: indeed, it is actually about a split personality. For Hitchcock, *Psycho* was a 'fun film', a technical exercise in audience manipulation, 'playing them', as he put it, 'like an organ'. The film is structured around three carefully spaced shocks: the murder in the motel shower of Marion Crane (Janet Leigh); the killing on the stairs of a detective (Martin Balsam) who is investigating the heroine's disappearance; and the final revelation in the cellar, when the skeleton of the mother is disturbed and the motel owner Norman Bates (Anthony Perkins) is revealed as the murderer. As Hitchcock planned, the biggest shock is the first, for several reasons: because it comes completely out of the blue; because a film does not normally kill off its heroine after only forty minutes; and because of its stylized impression of extraordinary violence, conveyed through exceptionally fast, imaginative editing and enhanced by the shrieking

violins of Bernard Herrmann's icily effective score. Afterwards, Hitchcock explained, the film becomes less violent but more tense, because the horror has been transferred into the mind of the audience.

But, acknowledging the genius with which Hitchcock accomplishes a collective apprehension in his audience, can one solely explain the impact of *Psycho* in terms of mechanistic manipulation and physical shock? The audience is drawn into the film's world very cleverly, but part of the fascination is surely that world itself, which is a very disturbing one. One of the major motifs is the chilling recurrence of 'dead' or 'sightless' eyes: the policeman's dark glasses, which terrify Marion and make him appear to her as a kind of Nemesis; the night eyes of the stuffed owls in Norman's room which seem to watch his every move; Marion's dead eye after the shower murder, signalling the end of her point of view; the eyeless sockets of the

mother at the end as the horrifying secret at the root of Norman's soul is wrenched out of the depths. It is a world of nihilism and neurosis, and Norman and Marion are characters in private traps, whose identities are to be swallowed up in a swamp of sexual guilt. Because Anthony Perkins and Janet Leigh give the performances of their lives, the personalities seem unusually sympathetic, their fates disproportionately hideous. *Psycho* is the *Macbeth* of the horror film, a slashing, blood-soaked journey into the dark vortex of madness and murder, where the host will murder his guest and then hope that a little water will clear him of this deed. Whether taken as black comedy or spiritual nightmare, *Psycho* is unforgettable, ensuring that the mysterious spirit of master film-maker Hitchcock will continue to grin menacingly and mischievously at us from beyond the grave – like Norman Bates's mummy.

LEFT: Marion Crane (Janet Leigh) has some sandwiches at the Bates Motel, whilst trying to decide whether to return the money she has stolen.

ABOVE: The famous shower scene. Janet Leigh screams as her assailant tears open the curtain and attacks her with a knife. Her screams are heightened by the terrifying sound of the 'screaming' violins in Bernard Herrmann's remarkable score. When asked why he did *Psycho*, Hitchcock replied that it was 'because of the suddenness of the murder in the shower, coming, as it were, out of nowhere'.

RIGHT: Disposing of the evidence. Norman Bates (Anthony Perkins) watches tensely as the car containing the girl's murdered body sinks into the swamp. The bleak landscape is consistent with the film's visual and emotional desolation.

BELOW: The private detective (Martin Balsam) questions Bates over the disappearance of Marion.

BOTTOM RIGHT: The film's final descent into darkness. Marion's sister, Lila (Vera Miles), prepares to enter the cellar, which holds the terrifying solution to the mystery.

ROMANCE

Camille (1937) · *The Prisoner of Zenda* (1937) ·
Gone With the Wind (1939) *Casablanca* (1943) ·
Les Enfants Du Paradis (1945) · *Brief Encounter* (1945)

As time goes by, the film-going public has always welcomed lovers. This was
never more true than during the late Thirties and early Forties when, with the
world clouded by war, audiences flocked to the cinema for a brief escape.
ABOVE: Robert Taylor kneels to screen goddess Greta Garbo in *Camille*.
LEFT: Scarlett O'Hara comes running from the verandah at Tara in the
opening scene of *Gone with the Wind*. She has just learned from the Tarleton
twins that Ashley Wilkes is going to marry Melanie Hamilton.

CAMILLE

USA 1937
DIRECTED BY GEORGE CUKOR

Producer: *Irving G. Thalberg*
Screenplay: *Zoe Akins,*
Frances Marion and James Hilton
Based on the novel and play,
La Dame aux Camelias by
Alexandre Dumas, *fils.*
Music: *Herbert Stothart*
Photography: *William Daniels and*
Karl Freund
MGM. 108 mins

Leading players: *Greta Garbo,*
Robert Taylor, Lionel Barrymore,
Henry Daniell, Jessie Ralph,
Laura Hope Crews.

Marguerite Gautier is a coughing courtesan in mid-19th century Paris, a lady whose love of camellias symbolizes her self-indulgent extravagance and her frivolous attitude to life. However, when she falls in love with a dashing young suitor, Armand, much to the displeasure of her former lover and protector, the Baron, she begins to re-evaluate her existence. Tragically, although her character improves, her consumptive illness does not. She dies with Armand at her bedside.

Dumas's famous story is a drama of contrasts – of luxury and love, of the corrupt glitter of the city and the moral wholesomeness of the country. Verdi's *La Traviata* converted it into grand opera; MGM's *Camille* transforms it into great Garbo. She has never been finer than here, intelligently suggesting Marguerite's recognition of the superficiality of the champagne society she adorns, and giving tremendous fervour to the character's desperate discovery of love at the moment when time is running out. Director George Cukor was fond of paying tribute to two particular Garbo gestures in the performance, which seemed to him moments of instinctive genius. There is the moment in the great scene with Armand's father (Lionel Barrymore) when her illusion of happiness is shattered by the realization that she must give up Armand and she suddenly sinks to the floor, one hand on the table, as if felled by Fate. There is also the moment when, having dropped her fan and the enraged Baron refuses to retrieve it for her, she picks it up herself without bending her knees, the physical refusal to stoop proclaiming a deep personal pride and her spirited defiance at the Baron's crude attempt at humiliation. There have been a few critics who have not succumbed to the Garbo mystique: 'sex on a high horse', one called her. But her performance as Marguerite has lightness and wit as well as poignant grandeur: it is one of the monuments of romantic cinema.

Cukor directs with that elegance of eroticism and sensitivity to surroundings that always distinguished his pictures; the costuming changes from white to grey to black convey the shifting moods with particular skill. Henry Daniell as the Baron plays with typical polished pomposity, and Robert Taylor's Armand has an impetuous ardour that seems appropriate and convincing. But, inevitably, supporting players in a Garbo film tend to look less like co-stars than extras. *Camille* belongs to its star. When asked to define star quality, Orson Welles said: 'There are just some people whom the camera loves.' During Garbo's exquisite death scene in *Camille*, the camera is stunned into stillness, as if the camera itself is paralysed with grief.

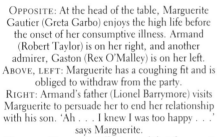

OPPOSITE: At the head of the table, Marguerite Gautier (Greta Garbo) enjoys the high life before the onset of her consumptive illness. Armand (Robert Taylor) is on her right, and another admirer, Gaston (Rex O'Malley) is on her left.

ABOVE, LEFT: Marguerite has a coughing fit and is obliged to withdraw from the party.

RIGHT: Armand's father (Lionel Barrymore) visits Marguerite to persuade her to end her relationship with his son. 'Ah . . . I knew I was too happy . . .' says Marguerite.

CENTRE: Marguerite tells Armand that they must part. He is unaware of the seriousness of her illness, and that his father has been to see her.

BELOW LEFT: Armand confronts Marguerite in the gaming rooms. Framed in the doorway are Gaston, Olympe (Leonore Ulric) and the Baron (Henry Daniell), Marguerite's former lover. Note Marguerite's dark gown, which reflects the darkening mood of the film and her increasingly tragic situation.

RIGHT: The final scene. Armand embraces the dying Marguerite.

THE PRISONER OF ZENDA

USA 1937
DIRECTED BY JOHN CROMWELL

Producer: *David O. Selznick*
Screenplay: *John Balderston,
Wills Root and
Donald Ogden Stewart*
Based on the novel by Anthony Hope
Music: *Alfred Newman*
Photography: *James Wong Howe*
Art Director: *Lyle Wheeler*
Selznick. 101 mins

Leading players:
*Ronald Colman,
Douglas Fairbanks Jr,
Madeleine Carroll, David Niven,
Raymond Massey, Mary Astor,
C. Aubrey Smith.*

ABOVE: The King's half-brother, Michael (Raymond Massey) and Rupert of Hentzau (Douglas Fairbanks Jr) hatch a plot against the King in Michael's study. LEFT: Rudolf Rassendyll (Ronald Colman) reacts initially with horror when asked to impersonate the King. BELOW: Disguised as the King at the Coronation, Rudolf receives advice from the King's aides, Colonel Zapt (C. Aubrey Smith) and Captain Fritz von Tarlenheim (David Niven). CENTRE: The 'King' and his Queen, Flavia (Madeleine Carroll). FAR RIGHT: Antoinette de Mauban (Mary Astor), who is in love with Michael, converses conspiratorially with Rupert of Hentzau. BOTTOM RIGHT: The brilliantly staged final duel between Hentzau and Rassendyll. In the tradition of all great swashbuckler films, it is as much a duel of words as swords. When he sees the game is up, Hentzau makes a characteristically stylish escape. 'This is getting too hot for me,' he says to Rassendyll. 'Au revoir, play-actor.'

Defining the appeal of the Romantic novel, Anthony Hope declared: 'The romance can give to love an ideal object, to ambition a boundless field, to courage a high occasion; and these great emotions, revelling in their freedom, exhibit themselves in their glory. Thus in its most

worthy forms, it can not only delight men but can touch them to the very heart.' In 1894, Hope had written one of the definitive examples of the form, *The Prisoner of Zenda*, about an Englishman, Rudolph Rassendyll, who bears an uncanny likeness to the ruler of Ruritania and who is called upon to impersonate the King when the latter is drugged and kidnapped by his half-brother Michael and the villainous Rupert of Hentzau. The story had been filmed twice in the silent era (by Edwin S. Porter in 1913, and by Rex Ingram in 1922) but the third version in 1937 is undoubtedly the greatest.

In his voluminous memoirs, producer David Selznick disclosed three reasons why he thought another version of *Zenda* was timely. He felt audiences were ready for a change from realism and for what he called a 'great and clean love story'. He also felt that the 'Windsor case', as he called it – Edward VIII's abdication of the throne because of his love for Mrs Simpson – made the subject of *Zenda* very topical, giving new life to the King and commoner theme. The most pressing reason perhaps was that he had Ronald Colman under contract and felt he would be ideal casting for the chivalrous Englishman, as indeed it proved.

Selznick would bring all kinds of diverse talents into his films if he felt they had some particular expertise he could use. The film's direction was shared between three people. Most of it was done by John Cromwell, selected for his taste and theatrical experience. The duel scenes were handled by the more rugged W. S.

Van Dyke, and Madeleine Carroll's key scenes were directed by George Cukor who, Selznick assured Colman, 'is one of the finest directors in the world'. (Ten years later, Colman was to win his Best Actor Oscar under Cukor's direction for *A Double Life*.)

Zenda proved to be a film in which the talents blended perfectly. Of the performers, one should perhaps single out Douglas Fairbanks Jr as Rupert of Hentzau, a rousing rendering of one of the most entertaining rogues of romantic fiction. Even allowing for the splendour of the Coronation and the Ball, the highlight of the film is the spectacular sword-fight between Rassendyll and Hentzau, with

each swashbuckling thrust punctuated by an equally sharp insult or quip.

For a story and film about imitation, it is ironic how much both have subsequently been imitated. The 1952 film remake (with Stewart Granger and James Mason) copies this version almost shot for shot. In his book, *Royal Flash*, George MacDonald Fraser appropriates Hope's plot for a very different picture of Victorian values. Fraser's dedication to this book reads: 'for Ronald Colman, Douglas Fairbanks Jr, Errol Flynn, Basil Rathbone, Louis Hayward, Tyrone Power, and all the rest of them.' A worthy list – and the noblest of them is Ronald Colman and *The Prisoner of Zenda*.

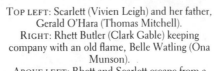

TOP LEFT: Scarlett (Vivien Leigh) and her father, Gerald O'Hara (Thomas Mitchell).
RIGHT: Rhett Butler (Clark Gable) keeping company with an old flame, Belle Watling (Ona Munson).
ABOVE LEFT: Rhett and Scarlett escape from a blazing Atlanta, taking Melanie and her baby. This scene had to be shot first to clear the way for the remaining sets. Note that Scarlett is in long shot. Vivien Leigh had not yet been cast.
LEFT: Rhett leaves Scarlett to make the rest of the way to Tara without him, whilst he goes off to fight in the war.

ABOVE: Scarlett kills an army deserter (Paul Hurst), bent on plunder, on the staircase at Tara, a scene directed by George Cukor.
TOP RIGHT: Believing Rhett to be a rich man Scarlett, badly in need of money, goest to Atlanta to find him. She discovers him in prison.
RIGHT: After the death of her second husband, Frank, Scarlett receives a proposal of marriage from Rhett.

GONE WITH THE WIND

USA 1939

DIRECTED BY
VICTOR FLEMING

Producer: *David O. Selznick*
Screenplay: *Sidney Howard*
Based on the novel by
Margaret Mitchell
Music: *Max Steiner*
Photography: *Ernest Haller,
Ray Rennahan*
Production Design:
William Cameron Menzies
MGM/Selznick. 220 mins

Leading players:
*Clark Gable, Vivien Leigh,
Leslie Howard,
Olivia de Havilland,
Thomas Mitchell,
Hattie McDaniel, Barbara O'Neil,
Ona Munson.*

Gone With the Wind achieved the impossible: it lived up to its own publicity. The novel is a saga of the destruction and reconstruction of the American South during and after the Civil War, and producer David Selznick had snapped up the screen rights before it had proved a runaway success. Determined to produce a film that would not only duplicate but surpass the book's popularity, he supervised every minute detail of colour, costume, music and design. The credits tell only half the story. Three directors participated (Cukor and Sam Wood worked on the film, in addition to the credited Fleming). The final script was the combined contribution of eight writers, including, at various stages, Ben Hecht and Scott Fitzgerald. A massive campaign to find the right actress to play Scarlett O'Hara had still not been concluded when the film started shooting.

Rhett Butler and Scarlett O'Hara are the Antony and Cleopatra of American romantic film folklore. Against the background of an aristocratic society that collapses and then struggles to be re-born, their love flickers, flames and then subsides. Rhett exhaustedly consigns Scarlett to damnation at the very moment when she has recognized her lifelong infatuation for Ashley Wilkes (Leslie Howard) as a false romantic illusion. In a sense, Wilkes is the villain of the piece: a man of gentility, married to the virtuous Melanie (Olivia De Havilland), yet encouraging Scarlett's feelings, but with no intention of fulfilling her wishes. His pallid nobility seems lankly unattractive beside Rhett's cheerful cynicism, just as Melanie's simple goodness is far less involving than Scarlett's self-seeking vitality.

With sweeping Steiner music and vividly expressive colour, the tangled emotions rise to fever-pitch, at times *The Taming of the Shrew*, at other times *War and Peace*. The devastation of war is eloquently shown in a single tracking shot in which Scarlet is almost lost from view amidst the sprawling bodies of the dead and wounded soldiers; and the burning of Atlanta (filmed first to clear the way for the other sets) is a set-piece of pulsating excitement. The use of the American South as an expressive setting for outsize emotions anticipated a whole train of American film and television melodrama, embracing such varied achievements as *Giant* (1956), *Mandingo* (1973) and even *Dallas*.

It was the public who had demanded that Clark Gable play the part of Rhett Butler: his performance amply repays that awesome trust. As Scarlett, Vivien Leigh is all feminine caprice and skilfully hooded intelligence, suggesting a potential somehow warped by the delusion that love should be the consuming goal of her life. (Intriguingly, the performance antici-

pates her definitive rendering of Blanche in Tennessee Williams's *A Streetcar named Desire*, another Southern belle of a later vintage, similarly clinging to romantic illusions as her property and body are violated.) *Gone With the Wind* might not be a masterpiece of screen art, but it is the quintessence of Hollywood entertainment, laying on its emotion and spectacle with an authority and conviction that defy anyone not to be overwhelmed. Would anybody *dare* to re-make it?

LEFT: Clark Gable as Rhett Butler, the public's choice for the rôle.
OPPOSITE, TOP: Mammy (Hattie McDaniel) receives Melanie (Olivia de Havilland) after the death of Bonnie.
BOTTOM: Ashley Wilkes (Leslie Howard) holds his son after the death of his wife, Melanie. Scarlett and Rhett watch, pensively.
BELOW: The wounded at the Atlanta depot. Scarlett is barely visible amidst the sprawling bodies.

CASABLANCA

USA 1943

DIRECTED BY
MICHAEL CURTIZ

Producer: *Hal B. Wallis*
Screenplay: *Julius J. Epstein,*
Philip G. Epstein and Howard Koch
Based on an unproduced play
Everybody Comes to Rick's by
Murray Burnett and Joan Alison
Music: *Max Steiner*
Photography: *Arthur Edeson*
Warner Brothers. 102 mins

Leading players:
Humphrey Bogart, Ingrid Bergman,
Claude Rains, Paul Henreid,
Conrad Veidt, Sydney Greenstreet,
Peter Lorre, Dooley Wilson.

Who would have thought that *Casablanca* would become a treasure of Hollywood melodrama? Certainly not the actors, who were complaining about the script while the film was being made, nor the writers, who were still writing the script while the cast was complaining. Yet this is one of those films in which everything works, even the ripest of romantic effects. When Rick (Humphrey Bogart) is jilted without explanation by Ilse (Ingrid Bergman), rain spatters down on the farewell letter, an eloquent simulation of tears and a sentimental metaphor for Rick's feeling of inner disintegration.

Ilse is the wife of freedom fighter Victor Laszlo (Paul Henreid). Thinking Laszlo had been killed, she had fallen in love with Rick in Paris, only to learn at the last moment that Laszlo was still alive and needed her. Now in the neutral territory of Casablanca, and being watched by the Nazi, Major Strasser (Conrad Veidt) and by the sardonic Chief of Police, Renault (Claude Rains), Laszlo and Ilse need Rick's help to get to America. 'I stick my neck out for nobody,' Rick says.

Casablanca as setting is a melting pot of various nationalities, personalities and opportunities, a place of transit, a personal purgatory, or a private retreat. Rick says he came for the waters. 'What waters? We're in the desert,' says Renault, to which Rick replies, laconically: 'I was misinformed.'

He has been a freedom fighter, but the film emphasizes his present state: emotionally bruised, wary of involvement. His gradual entanglement with the political situation in Casablanca springs from individual more than ideological causes.

'Casablanca' in Spanish means 'white house' and the film has sometimes been interpreted as an allegory of America's involvement in the war, with Rick a surrogate of Roosevelt whose isolationism is ultimately transformed into action. The action takes place during December 1941, the month of Pearl Harbor. Nowadays, the political allegory looks almost irrelevant. *Casablanca* is remembered for 'As Time Goes By', for the drowning of the Horst Wessel song by the *Marseillaise*, and for its apotheosis of Bogart's world-weary stoicism and Ingrid Bergman's tremulous pathos. The final airport scene is more about 'the fight for love and glory' than the fight against Fascism, and the gestures of noble renunciation are romantic more than real; as a critic remarked, the way we wanted to be rather than the way we were. *Casablanca* won its best film Oscar for its timely message of commitment, but, as with most great Hollywood films, the magic counts for more than the message.

LEFT: 'I like it fine here.' Sam (Dooley Wilson, at piano) refuses the offer of a higher salary from Ferrari (Sydney Greenstreet), preferring to continue working for Rick (Humphrey Bogart).

ABOVE: A confrontation between Major Strasser (Conrad Veidt, second from left) and Victor Laszlo (Paul Henreid, second from right), watched by Captain Renault (Claude Rains, left) and Ilse Laszlo (Ingrid Bergman).

TOP RIGHT: Ugarte (Peter Lorre) cashes in his chips after being arrested by the police.

RIGHT: Rick pulls a gun on Renault as part of his plan to help Laszlo and Ilse escape from Casablanca.

BELOW: Rick and Ilse try to sort out their emotional problems. 'You'll have to think for both of us,' she tells him, 'for all of us.'

BOTTOM RIGHT: The final scene at the airport. Major Strasser tries to prevent the plane from departing.

LES ENFANTS DU PARADIS

FRANCE 1945
DIRECTED BY MARCEL CARNÉ

Producer: *Fred Orain*
Screenplay: *Jacques Prévert*
Photography: *Roger Hubert*
Music: *Joseph Kosma and
Maurice Thiriet*
195 mins

Leading players:
*Arletty, Jean-Louis Barrault,
Pierre Brasseur, Marcel Herrand,
Maria Casarès, Pierre Renoir,
Louis Salou*

No film was ever more stagestruck than *Les Enfants du Paradis*. Its world is a stage and its theme the tension between Art and Life. When he finds he is jealous in reality, the great actor Frederic Lemaître (Pierre Brasseur) can transfer this feeling into his playing of Othello. Conversely, the mime Baptiste (Jean-Louis Barrault), acting the part of the defeated lover on stage, looks backstage to find his art anticipating his experience in life.

The idea for the film originated with Barrault, who suggested a film about the celebrated nineteenth-century French mime, Baptiste Debureau, because he was intrigued by the concept of putting a mime in a talkie. Writer Jacques Prévert reworked the characters, making Baptiste one of four men enraptured by the beauty of Garance (Arletty). With director Marcel Carné, he was also determined to make full use of the setting of the *Boulevard du Crime* – the area in which Baptiste lived and which was a nest of thieves and murderers – and of the Funambules, the theatre at which Baptiste worked, to the particular delight of the people in the *Paradis* (the lower-class audience up in the 'gods').

Set in the Romantic Paris of the 1840s, *Les Enfants du Paradis* could be described as the cinema's equivalent of Berlioz's *Symphonie Fantastique*, a story of obsessive love told in the heightened language of French Romanticism. It is a world of grand gestures and emotional extremes, with star roles for a tragic clown and a clownish tragedian, for a quarrelsome aristocrat and a gentleman criminal. It is a film which explores the varieties of love, from the romantic fatalism of Baptiste to the Iago-like embittered possessiveness of the murderer Lacenaire (a splendid performance from Marcel Herrand). Whereas Baptiste's wife Natalie (Maria Casarès) represents one-dimensional love in all its solid, dogged devotion, Garance is love at its most unfettered, illusory and elusive, finally disappearing into the distance, chased helplessly by the idealist Baptiste through a mockingly cheerful, carnival world of confetti and masks.

Watching the splendid performances and the exquisite tact of Carné's direction, one might find it hard to remember that the film was made under desperate conditions over a period of three years during the German Occupation of France in World War II. Its quintessentially French elegance seems to transcend mere aesthetic triumph: it is an act of nationalistic pride and defiance. During the youthful, impetuous, improvisatory heyday of the French *nouvelle vague* in the late Fifties and Sixties, it was a kind of cinema that fell out of fashion: theatrical, artificial, soberly calculated, literary. But quality, although it can occasionally become unfashionable, can never truly date. In 1979, the French film Academy was to vote *Les Enfants du Paradis* the 'best French film of all time'.

OPPOSITE, TOP: The children of the *paradis*, the people who crowd the gods to admire the work of Baptiste Debureau. BOTTOM: On stage at the Funambules. Baptiste (Jean-Louis Barrault) mimes his love for the cool figure in the pose and costume of the goddess Diana. She is Garance (Arletty). LEFT: Natalie (Maria Casarès) tries to console Baptiste, who has fallen in love with Garance. He marries Natalie when Garance goes away. BELOW: A reunion at the Funambules years later. Garance and the great actor Lemaître (Pierre Brasseur), one of the four men in the story romantically involved with her. BOTTOM LEFT: The criminal, Lacenaire (Marcel Herrand), confronts the Comte de Montray (Louis Salou). Garance has become the Comte's mistress and Lacenaire's jealousy grows more bitter. RIGHT: The final scene. Garance departs after a bitter outburst from Natalie, and disappears into the carnival crowds. Baptiste pursues her hopelessly, the teeming masks of jollity counterpointing his despair.

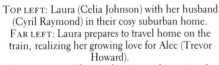

BRIEF ENCOUNTER

G.B. 1945
DIRECTED BY DAVID LEAN

Producer: *Noël Coward*
Screenplay: *Noël Coward*
Based on his one-act play, *Still Life*,
from the collection,
Tonight at 8.30
Music:
Rachmaninov Piano Concerto No. 2
Photography: *Robert Krasker*
86 mins

Leading players:
*Celia Johnson, Trevor Howard,
Stanley Holloway, Cyril Raymond,
Joyce Cary.*

'Make tea, not love,' was the critic Raymond Durgnat's summary of the emotional temperature of this film. It is certainly strange that the greatest love story in the British cinema – which *Brief Encounter* indisputably is – should be about unconsummated passion and in which nothing actually 'happens'. Nevertheless, still waters run deep, and the restraint of *Brief Encounter* contains a reservoir of deep feeling.

The situation is simple. A middle-class housewife Laura (Celia Johnson) briefly encounters a doctor, Alec (Trevor Howard) at the local station when a piece of grit gets in her eye. They fall in love but both are married. When Alec is offered a job in Johannesburg, they part, leaving Laura to go back to her marriage. An ordinary, even banal, story, why does it exert such mesmerizing power? Because of the way the story is told and who tells it. It is narrated by Laura, in a state of shock, after returning home from the parting with Alec.

Almost everything is seen through Laura's eyes and, because of this, the film has enormous concentration and intensity. What we are being given through Laura's narration is an unconscious self-portrait. Possibly without realizing it herself, Laura is a deeply romantic person, a fact revealed gradually through the books she reads, the music she enjoys, the films she sees (*Love in a Mist*), the poetry she loves. When her husband is stumped for the missing word in his *Times* crossword, Laura can supply it: 'Romance' (for her husband, the word is only 'something – in seven letters'). Through such details, and through Celia Johnson's exquisite performance, we sense a potentially passionate side to Laura that her comfortable life has barely begun to satisfy. Yet the pressures of conformity are so strong that, as soon as these deeper feelings begin to surface, they are accompanied by an overwhelming sense of guilt and shame. David Lean's films – especially *Great Expectations* (1946) and *Ryan's Daughter* (1969) – will often return to the theme of frustrated romance, the longing for passion and yet the fear of its consequences.

Rachmaninov's concerto surges over the soundtrack as an overpowering accompaniment to the heroine's reverie. With this Russian music, it is almost as if Laura thinks of herself as an English Anna Karenina, but within English constraints that stop short of total abandonment: unlike Tolstoy's heroine, Laura *almost* commits adultery, *almost* leaves her children, *almost* commits suicide by throwing herself under a train. But it is no wonder she is so distraught at the end. The swirlings of romance – the sense of a vital world outside of the one she had created for herself and thought she wanted – have undermined the structure of her existence. What is there for her in the future? With compassion and precision, Noël Coward and David Lean have laid bare a whole set of values, a whole way of life. A seemingly drab suburban drama is given the intensity of a fevered, subversive dream.

TOP LEFT: Laura (Celia Johnson) with her husband (Cyril Raymond) in their cosy suburban home.
FAR LEFT: Laura prepares to travel home on the train, realizing her growing love for Alec (Trevor Howard).
CENTRE LEFT: After an abortive rendezvous at the flat of Alec's friend, Laura flees and sits desolate on a park bench, wracked by guilt.
LEFT: The final meeting between Alec and Laura in the railway buffet is interrupted by the unwelcome appearance of Laura's insensitive and gossipy friend, Dolly (Everley Gregg). 'My dear, what a nice looking man,' Dolly says to Laura as Alec gets her a cup of tea. 'Really, you're quite a dark horse.'
RIGHT: Laura's last sight of Alec, as he leaves to catch his train.
TOP RIGHT: Laura's face reflects panic and pain as the full impact of Alec's departure hits her. In a moment she will leave the buffet and, for a second, contemplate throwing herself under a train.

WAR

All Quiet on the Western Front (1930) ·
La Grande Illusion (1937) · *Rome – Open City* (1945) ·
The Wajda Trilogy (1955–8).

The great war films seem to be those which express a hatred of war, and pity
for the young men whose lives will be sacrificed. This is particularly true of the
two films illustrated.
LEFT: The soldiers sing in the dug-out in *All Quiet on the Western Front*.
ABOVE: Maciek (Zbigniew Cybulski) makes a horrifying discovery in the
chapel in *Ashes and Diamonds*.

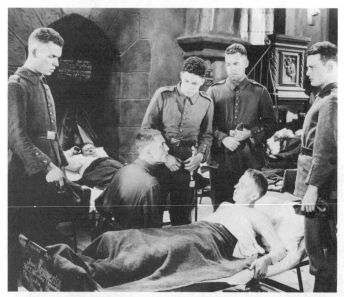

Top left: Flushed with patriotism and dreams of glory, the young boys enlist. Here they are addressed by Sergeant Himmelstoss (John Wray) who was formerly their postman.
Centre left: Muller (Russell Gleason) asks the dying Kemmerich (Ben Alexander) if he can have his boots. Paul (Lew Ayres, right) is shocked by this insensitivity.
Left: The two friends, the sly veteran Katczinsky (Louis Wolheim) and the young recruit Paul converse about the war.
Above: Paul bayonets a French soldier (Raymond Griffith), but then feels an anguished kinship with the man he has killed. 'Forgive me, comrade, how could you be my enemy?'
Right: The battlefield.
Top right: Paul reaches towards a butterfly: his hand stiffens and then jerks back as he is hit by a sniper's bullet. 'This is one piece you cannot finish with a crescendo,' said director Lewis Milestone. 'You cannot top the whole piece.'

ALL QUIET ON THE WESTERN FRONT

USA 1930

DIRECTED BY
LEWIS MILESTONE

Producer: *Carl Laemmle Jr.*
Screenplay: *Maxwell Anderson,
George Abbott and Del Andrews.*
Based on the novel by
Erich Maria Remarque
Photography: *Arthur Edeson*
Dialogue director: *George Cukor*
Universal. 140 mins

Leading players:
*Lew Ayres, Louis Wolheim,
John Wray.*

In his preface to *All Quiet on the Western Front*, Erich Maria Remarque described the novel as 'neither an accusation nor a confession, and least of all an adventure. It will try simply to tell of a generation who were destroyed by the war.' A story of young Germans in the First World War, it details the gradual erosion of their idealism to bitterness and despair as they move from parade-ground to battlefield.

The film of *All Quiet on the Western Front* reproduces the novel's fierce anti-war sentiment with few compromises. Nowadays perhaps some of the dialogue scenes creak a bit and the issues seem oversimplified. Nevertheless, the fact that the film has been revived so often since its original release date testifies to a basic truth, a convincing hatred of war, to which audiences always respond. The battle scenes – those raking, stomach-churning panning shots of unceasing, uninhibited carnage – remain unsurpassed. At the time, Graham Greene regarded them as a 'permanent encouragement to those who believe that an art may yet emerge from a popular industry'.

The tone is sometimes grimly humorous. The young German recruits are dismayed to discover that their soft village postman has transformed himself into a sadistic drill-sergeant. A dying soldier's last wish is that his soft leather boots should be passed on. In a grisly montage of mordant humour, we see that these boots are indeed passed on – and on and on . . .

Mostly the feeling is one of an ashen disillusionment. During a fierce shelling attack, a young German soldier, Paul Baumer (Lew Ayres) dives into a crater and, in terror, plunges his bayonet into a Frenchman. As he sits trapped with his victim, his terror turns to remorse. 'Forgive me, comrade,' he says, 'How could you be my enemy?' This tortured sense of common humanity, trapped in a world of murderous insanity, is a feeling often to be found in the great Great War poetry of Wilfred Owen and Siegfried Sassoon. The film is similarly hostile to the politicians and commanders who can sanction such slaughter; and horrified at the gap between the reality of war and the romantic notions of it at home. When Paul returns home, he is asked by his eager schoolmaster to tell the pupils what it is really like on the Front. 'We live in the trenches,' he says, with bleak bitterness. 'We fight. We try not to get killed. That's all.'

The director felt that the ending of the film might be a problem, for this was one work which could not finish on a crescendo: the tone and theme demanded a diminuendo of despair. The solution is the film's most famous moment. During a lull in the fighting, Paul spots a butterfly outside his dug-out. He reaches out his hand to something beautiful and unsullied; a sniper sees the movement, and, as the sound of a bullet is heard, the outstretched hand stiffens, jerks back and then falls limp. It is the definitive image of war as a violation of Nature, and of human nature.

LEFT: Maréchal (Jean Gabin) talks to Captain de Boieldieu (Pierre Fresnay) in the prisoner of war camp. Maréchal has been piloting a plane carrying de Boieldieu, which has been shot down by the Germans.
BELOW: The camp concert with English officers in drag. Julien Carette (centre) is drawn into the performance.
BOTTOM: The prisoners work on the escape tunnel. *Clockwise*: Jean Gabin, Gaston Modot, Marcel Dalio, Jean Dasté, Julien Carette in the hole. The day before the completion of the tunnel, the prisoners are told they are to be moved.
OPPOSITE, TOP: de Boieldieu is shot by von Rauffenstein as he assists in the break-out.
BOTTOM, LEFT: Captain von Rauffenstein (Erich von Stroheim) says farewell to the dying de Boieldieu, both recognizing that their common code of chivalry has no longer any place in modern warfare.
RIGHT: On the run, Maréchal and Rosenthal (Marcel Dalio) are sheltered by a German farm woman, Elsa (Dita Parlo), who is to fall in love with Maréchal.

LA GRANDE ILLUSION

FRANCE 1937
DIRECTED BY JEAN RENOIR

Producers: *Frank Rollmer, Albert Pinkovitch*
Screenplay: *Charles Spaak and Jean Renoir*
Music: *Joseph Kosma*
Photography: *Christian Matras*
114 mins

Leading players:
Jean Gabin, Erich von Stroheim, Pierre Fresnay, Marcel Dalio, Dita Parlo.

La Grande Illusion is one of the most famous and popular of war films, yet there are no scenes of battle in it. The film is chiefly concerned with the relationship between French and English prisoners and their German captors in World War I. Amidst the occasional camp humour (a Christmas party, with English officers in drag) and the occasional tragedy (the shooting of a French officer who is assisting an attempt to escape), the film is a study of friendship between men and the instinctive individual thirst for freedom which compels the prisoners to attempt to break out of the camp time after time.

In the film, Renoir explores a theme that has always fascinated him: the idea, as he says, that the world is not divided vertically by frontier but horizontally by class and calling. If true, it makes war an absurdity. In *La Grande Illusion*, this means that the French officer de Boieldieu (Pierre Fresnay) has less in common with his fellow Frenchmen than with his equally aristocratic German captor, von Rauffenstein (Erich von Stroheim). The two nominal adversaries strike up a deep mutual respect, borne of a recognition that their way of life is dying. Erich von Stroheim imparts a melancholy magnificence to the role of von Rauffenstein, with every detail (the white gloves, the riding crop, the chin brace) proclaiming an ingrained discipline and fastidiousness.

Two of the prisoners, Maréchal (Jean Gabin) and Rosenthal (Marcel Dalio) escape and, for a while, are sheltered by a

German widow. Love grows between Maréchal and the woman (Dita Parlo), again demonstrating the possibility of mutual human feeling transcending barriers of nationalism and language. However, they must part as the two Frenchmen make a bid for freedom and, in a famous final shot, Maréchal and Rosenthal become two almost indistinct black figures, barely perceptible against a background of snow as they head into Switzerland towards an uncertain future.

The title of the film has numerous different implications. As François Truffaut has remarked, von Rauffenstein and de Boieldieu share a *grande illusion* that war can still be fought on chivalric lines. For Maréchal and Rosenthal, the *grande illusion* is freedom itself: at the end, we are not sure they have attained it, but we are sure that it is a goal they will always seek, however elusive. An illusion that the film tries precariously to affirm is that the First World War might also possibly be the last. Maybe a pacifist film in the 1930s could still make a difference to world history. 'I overestimated the power of the cinema,' Renoir commented later. 'The film, for all its success, did not prevent the Second World War.' Nevertheless, its humanity and idealism, if ultimately illusory amidst the encircling barbarism, stemmed from the noblest of human motives: the refusal to accept that people must hate each other. In the hands of a Renoir, cinema itself becomes a grand illusion.

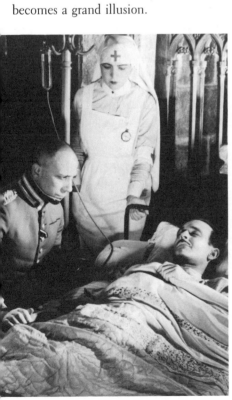

ITALY 1945

DIRECTED BY ROBERTO ROSSELLINI

Screenplay: *Sergio Amidei, Federico Fellini and Robert Rossellini*
Based on a story by Sergio Amidei and Alberto Consiglio
Music: *Renzo Rossellini*
Photography: *Ubaldo Arata*
100 mins

Leading players:
Anna Magnani, Aldo Fabrizi, Marcello Pagliero.

TOP: The return of the children to the city.
ABOVE: The Gestapo spy, Ingrid (Giovanna Galletti), in a scene with Major Bergmann (Harry Feist).
RIGHT: The priest Don Pietro (Aldo Fabrizzi). He is on the side of the Resistance and is to sacrifice his life for them.
OPPOSITE, TOP: The Gestapo search the workers' flats.
BOTTOM LEFT: The vibrant femininity of Pina (Anna Magnani) contrasts with the sterile detachment of the spy Ingrid.
FAR RIGHT: Pina's fiancée is arrested and, in chasing after the Gestapo lorry, Pina is shot. This uncompromising moment reflects the film's refusal to sentimentalize or distort reality. 'The war was a decisive period for us all,' said Vittorio de Sica, on behalf of his fellow Italian film-makers. 'Each of us felt the urge to sweep away all the worn-out plots and set up our cameras in the midst of real life, in the midst of all that struck us with dismay.'

Roberto Rossellini's *Rome – Open City* was born out of the ashes of the War, written during the German occupation, shot immediately after the Allies had liberated Rome, and has the authority and passion of first-hand authentic experience. The plot is fictional but has the conviction of documentary. A Resistance leader on the run from the Gestapo is betrayed, tortured and killed. The friend who has harboured him is hauled away by the police, the friend's fiancée (Anna Magnani) being shot as she gives chase after the Gestapo lorry – one of the most harrowing and heart-rending scenes in any war film. A priest who has assisted the Resistance is shot by a firing squad. Because of the angry passion of performance and style, the film has enormous presence and immediacy; recent history seems to be told in the present tense.

The film's sense of raw reality has, of course, much to do with the conditions under which it was made. It was shot on the actual locations, because all the studios had been destroyed – indeed, some of it was shot in the flat of one of the actresses. Rossellini and Magnani sold some of their clothes to raise money for the film stock, and the equipment was so primitive that the sound had to be post-synchronized. Yet, in this case, dreadful conditions and artistic intention seem to have beneficially fed off each other.

Maybe it would have been completely

impossible to reproduce the sheer conviction of this film under more controlled and artificial conditions; certainly the absence of producers and the usual industrial organization gave Rossellini complete aesthetic freedom. The mingling of non-actors with professional actors might not have been necessary in less straitened circumstances, but it is hard to avoid the conclusion that this conjunction was entirely to the film's advantage, the non-professionals giving the professionals a measure of 'reality' against which to test themselves.

The film's 'neo-realist' method, as it was called – among other things, involving a mixture of professional and non-professional players, location shooting, low budgets, the attempt to reflect 'real life' – was to prove immediately influential, locally and internationally. Out of it was to come the famous post-war films of de Sica, *Shoeshine* and *Bicycle Thieves*, and a short-lived post-war era of Hollywood realism that was to be seen in such film-makers as Elia Kazan and Fred Zinnemann. Its legacy lingers still in the ciné-verité, drama-doc styles of much modern film and (especially) television.

But Rossellini always said that, for him, 'neo-realism' was not really a style but an attitude, a 'moral standpoint from which to view the world'. The film is basically the story of a city: its poverty and pride, its spirit and potential re-birth symbolized through the courage by which people of different persuasions – Communist and Catholic – choose to unite in a common struggle against evil. The method is the means by which that urgent message can be expressed as powerfully and as movingly as possible.

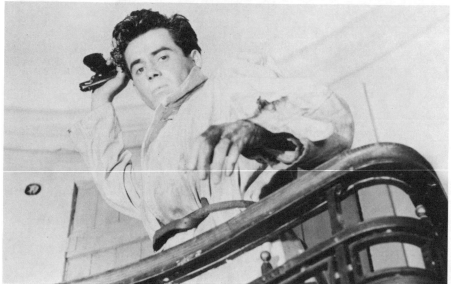

POLAND
DIRECTED BY
ANDRZEJ WAJDA

A GENERATION (1955)
Screenplay: *Bohdan Czeszko*.
Based on his novel.
Music: *Andrzej Markowski*.
Photography: *Jerzy Lipman*.
90 mins.
Leading players: *Urzula Modrzynska,
Tadeusz Lomnicki, Januz Palusziewicz,
Roman Polanski*.

KANAL (1957)
Screenplay: *Jerzy Stefan Stawinski*.
Music: *Jan Krenz*.
Photography: *Jerzy Lipman*.
97 mins.
Leading players: *Teresa Izewska,
Tadeusz Janczar*.

ASHES AND DIAMONDS (1958)
Screenplay: *Andrzej Wajda,
Jerzy Andrzejewski*.
Based on the novel by
Jerzy Andrzejewski.
Photography: *Jerzy Wojcik*.
106 mins.
Leading players:
Zbigniew Cybulski, Ewa Krzyzewska.

TOP: To the horror of his mother, Stach (Tadeusz Lomnicki) reveals that he has a pistol hidden under his cap. From *A Generation*.
ABOVE: Pursued by the Nazis up a staircase, Janek (Tadeusz Janczar) pauses to hurl his gun down at them, prior to his suicide. A scene from *A Generation*.
RIGHT: Korab (Tadeusz Janczar) and Stokrotka (Teresa Izewska, right) take refuge in the sewers of Warsaw. From *Kanal*.
CENTRE: 'Fresh air at last': Kula (Tadeusz Gwiaderowski), covered in slime, crawls out through the manhole. From *Kanal*.
TOP RIGHT: The banquet in *Ashes and Diamonds*. Drewnowski (Bogumil Kobiela) guns everyone in sight with the foam from a fire extinguisher.
CENTRE RIGHT: The lovers, Krystyna (Ewa Krzyewska) and Maciek (Zbigniew Cybulski) in *Ashes and Diamonds*.
BOTTOM RIGHT: Maciek, moaning and coughing like a wounded animal, expires on the rubbish heap. From *Ashes and Diamonds*.

It is a critical convention to group the first three feature films of the Polish director, Andrzej Wajda, as a 'trilogy', even though they were not planned as such. For, if they are not united by a common group of characters, they are united by a common theme: the nobility, courage and suffering of the Polish people during the Nazi occupation of World War II. Wajda was thirteen when the war broke out and three years later joined the Resistance. The films are an intensely felt reflection on what the war meant in personal and national terms.

A Generation follows the development of an adolescent during the war years, a growth symbolized by the hero's involvement with Resistance groups, his growing political awareness and his gradual assumption of leadership. However, it is the supporting characters one principally remembers. In those moments when the girl the hero loves is arrested, or a friend commits suicide rather than submit to arrest (a stunningly shot scene on a spiral staircase that twists higher and higher until a barred window conclusively blocks the boy's escape), one feels that apprehension of premature death which Wajda recalled as the one dominant emotion of those war years. In *Kanal*, the existence of those Resistance fighters who took refuge in the sewers of Warsaw after the failure of the 1944 uprising is explicitly likened by Wajda to Dante's Inferno. Their fate provides the substance of a bitter, uncompromising film.

Wajda's international reputation was firmly consolidated by *Ashes and Diamonds*, a brilliant thriller that portrays the political confusion of Poland at the end of the war. More than in the previous two films, Wajda seizes the opportunity to infuse the conflict with imaginative imag-

ery – the counterpoint of violent action with images of nature and religion, the observation of bizarre details (ants on a machine gun, a man's jacket bursting into flames after he is shot in the back) that gives a sharp immediacy to the drama. The film is especially memorable for a charismatic performance from Zbigniew Cybulski as a hero whose assignment to assassinate a communist leader is complicated by his unexpectedly falling in love, which completely shakes the direction of his life. The hero is being offered a choice literally between love and death, and his romantic anguish seems to symbolize the agony of a nation as it emerged apprehensively from a traumatic immediate past into an uncertain immediate future.

There is a lot of Wajda in *Ashes and Diamonds* – a romantic in an unromantic world, a man attempting to assert his own individuality against the pressure of the State and the forces of history. It has been said that film-makers in Poland are the nation's conscience and its public moralists. No one has undertaken that role with more craftsmanship and conviction than Andrzej Wajda. Three decades on from *A Generation*, he remains – by far – the finest film-maker the country has ever produced and one of the most distinguished in Europe.

CONTROVERSY

To Be or Not To Be (1942) · *Viridiana* (1961)
Andrei Rublev (1966) · *Weekend* (1967) ·
A Clockwork Orange (1971)

'If you wish to avoid criticism,' said the composer Jean Sibelius, 'say nothing,
do nothing – be nothing.' All the film-makers in this section have risked
public, critical and sometimes political disapproval in following through the
courage of their artistic convictions.
ABOVE: A young woman (Sylvia Pinal) is drugged by an old man (Fernando
Rey) in *Viridiana*. 'The whole work flowed from that image, like a fountain,'
said director Luis Buñuel.
LEFT: The bell-casting scene from *Andrei Rublev*. Nikolai Burljaev as the boy.

TO BE
OR NOT TO BE

USA 1942
DIRECTED BY ERNST LUBITSCH

Producers: *Ernst Lubitsch,
Alexander Korda*
Screenplay: *Edwin Justus Mayer*
Based on a story by Melchior
Lengyel and Ernst Lubitsch
Music: *Werner Heymann*
Photography: *Rudolph Maté*
United Artists. 99 mins

Leading players:
*Jack Benny, Carole Lombard,
Robert Stack, Sig Rumann,
Felix Bressart.*

On the face of it, to accuse that supremely sophisticated director, Ernst Lubitsch, of 'bad taste' would be like accusing Shakespeare of writing bad verse. Yet this is what happened to *To Be or Not To Be*, one of Lubitsch's last comedies in a career that had started in Germany during the silent period and included such expert Hollywood comedies as *Trouble in Paradise* (1932) and *Ninotchka* (1939). These had charmed critics and public alike, but in the words of one critic, *To Be or Not To*

Be was 'a callous, tasteless effort to find fun in the bombing of Warsaw'.

Admittedly, the material was provocative. From a story of a group of actors attempting to escape from occupied Poland, Lubitsch dares to make a comedy out of World War II. An actor plays Hitler in a production called 'Gestapo' and greets cries of 'Heil Hitler!' with a casual 'Heil myself'. Sig Rumann plays a Nazi purring delightedly over his nickname of 'Concentration Camp Ehrhardt'. Jack Benny plays the 'greatest Shakespearian actor in Poland', Joseph Tura, who, disguised as a Nazi collaborator, asks Ehrhardt for his opinion of Tura's talents. 'What he did to Shakespeare,' replies Ehrhardt, 'we are doing to Poland.' For some, this joke about Poland crossed the border from comedy to cruelty.

Lubitsch was stung into defending himself publicly from such criticism. He denied saying anything derogatory about Poles or Poland in the film (the newsreels of devastation are serious enough) and defended the film as a satire both on the 'ridiculous ideology' of the Nazis and on actors. It is certainly one of the great comedies about the theatre, about the vanity of actors and their inability to separate illusion from reality. Jack Benny

and Carole Lombard (as Tura's wife) have never been funnier on film (tragically, Miss Lombard was to be killed in an aircrash before the film was released).

However, Lubitsch's real subject is not the theatre itself, but the theatre of war. Perhaps in theme and method, the film was anticipated by Chaplin's masterly anti-Nazi tract, *The Great Dictator* (1940), yet Lubitsch's work is equally individual in a different way. Black comedy has perhaps become the most appropriate dramatic form for the heedless destructiveness of the twentieth century, and is generated by the feeling that some things are too serious to be taken seriously. Behind the laughter of *To Be or Not To Be* (as behind the humour of Joseph Heller's great comic war novel, *Catch-22*, or Stanley Kubrick's satirical film, *Dr. Strangelove*), there is a civilized but withering anger. The visuals recall Fritz Lang in their dark claustrophobia. Lubitsch was not a man given to strident denunciation. His deep outrage at Nazism and its devastation of his beloved Europe is expressed entirely characteristically: he holds it up to ridicule. It might not be the orthodox or the 'tasteful' thing to do. But, as Picasso said: 'Good taste is the enemy of art.'

OPPOSITE, TOP LEFT: The Nazis arrive in Warsaw.
TOP RIGHT: Carole Lombard as the actress, Maria Tura, courted by the Nazis but secretly working for the Polish underground.
CENTRE: On the instructions of Professor Siletsky, who is a Nazi spy, Maria Tura (Carole Lombard) is brought to Gestapo headquarters. 'As an actress it is important you choose the right part,' she is told, 'but in real life it is even more important that you choose the right side.'
BOTTOM: Masquerading as Colonel Ehrhardt, Tura (Jack Benny, right) prepares to meet the spy, Siletsky. Dobosh (Charles Halton, centre) and the aviator (Robert Stack, second from right) beg Tura not to drag out the scene.
TOP: Having outwitted the Nazis, the actors arrive in triumph in England. Tura takes credit for the success of the enterprise.
ABOVE: A Nazi in a haystack? Bronski (Tom Dugan) startles the British in his disguise as Hitler.

VIRIDIANA

SPAIN 1961
DIRECTED BY LUIS BUÑUEL

Producer: *Gustavo Alatriste*
Screenplay: *Luis Buñuel and
Jorge Alejandro*
Music: *Handel*
Photography: *Jose F. Aguayo*
90 mins

Leading players:
*Silvia Pinal, Fernando Rey,
Francisco Rabal,
Margarita Lozano.*

If *Fantasia* offended music lovers by its treatment of the classics, one can imagine what such people would have made of the massacre of Handel's *Messiah* in *Viridiana*. But we are a long way from Walt Disney. The Hallelujah Chorus in *Viridiana* accompanies an orgy by beggars who have overrun a house in the master's absence. At one moment, in one of the crispest visual coups in film history, they are frozen by Buñuel into a grouping that parodies Leonardo da Vinci's *The Last Supper*. The scene's assault on high culture and religious sensibility is inimitably the work of Luis Buñuel, for whom the cinema existed in order to outrage and offend conventional feeling. 'Thank God I'm an atheist,' he said, as he savaged religious orthodoxy and bourgeois moral-

TOP LEFT: Viridiana's cousin, Jorge (Francisco Rabal), with his mistress, Lucia (Victoria Zinny). After the suicide of his uncle, Jorge will join Viridiana to take charge of his house and farm.
CENTRE LEFT: Don Jamie (Fernando Rey) talks to his niece Viridiana (Sylvia Pinal), a convent-girl who is visiting him before taking her final vows and who arouses his lust. Note the contrast between Viridiana's plain robe and the ornate fireplace, with its erotic statuettes.
LEFT: As an act of religious charity, Viridiana lays on a feast for the local beggars.
TOP RIGHT: While the cats are away . . . When Jorge and Viridiana have to go into town on business, the beggars break into the house, ransacking the furnishings and clothing.
RIGHT: Buñuel's blasphemous tableau of The Last Supper. Before Viridiana and Jorge return the party will have degenerated into an orgy.

ity, both of which he regarded as deeply immoral.

The beggars' revolt in this film is the final defeat for Viridiana (Silvia Pinal), a novitiate who has postponed taking her final vows after her uncle's death and tried to help the needy in her community by instilling them with her own Christian values. Her attempt at leading beggars in prayer is sardonically crosscut with the activities of her cousin (Francisco Rabal), who has undertaken the task of renovating his father's property. His secular practicality is constantly contrasted to Viridiana's spiritual piety. Although the contrast is not a simple one (the cousin's predatory selfishness is no more laudable than Viridiana's naive generosity), Buñuel sees that Viridiana's attempt to live the life of Christ in modern society is doomed to failure. Her experience is a violent purgation of religious belief, but this might, providentially, have equipped her better for life. After inspecting herself in a mirror and letting her hair down, Viridiana surprises her cousin by joining him and the maid in his room and settling down for a game of cards.

The circumstances of the making of *Viridiana* are mysterious. After official outrage at two earlier films of his, *L'Age D'Or* (1930) and *Land Without Bread* (1932), Buñuel had been in exile from Spain for nearly thirty years. A Spanish producer had invited him back in 1960 to make *Viridiana*. Although Buñuel had submitted the required draft of his screenplay to the authorities, their only suggested revision was to tone down the original ending, a suggestion which the director felt actually helped the subversive impact of the final film. The insolence of the film's anti-authoritarian, anti-clerical tone in Franco's Spain seems only belatedly to have dawned. Although the film was suppressed in its own country, it won the Golden Palm award at Cannes and was

a huge international success. For most critics, the film's impish, menacing imagery (phallic skipping-rope handles, a crucifix that conceals a stiletto, the cat that jumps on the mouse as the cousin seduces the maid, Ramona) marked the return of Buñuel to his sly, surrealist form. *Viridiana* launched him on an immensely productive last phase of his career, making films that, as always, aimed to convince an affronted audience that, in Buñuel's words, 'they do not live in the best of all possible worlds'.

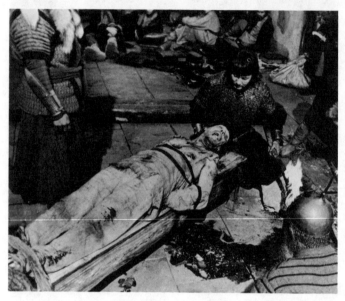

TOP LEFT: The Tartars on the rampage in medieval Russia, storming the city of Vladimir.

ABOVE: A man is tortured by the Tartars in a church, one of the many scenes of brutality against which Rublev's artistry and spirituality are contrasted.

ABOVE RIGHT: The Tartar chief in the church, surrounded by holy icons. The image captures the conflict between barbarity and beauty which animates the film's style and its portrayal of the tensions in the main character.

RIGHT: A society in turmoil, subject to peremptory forces. An angry crowd watch an arrest.

FAR RIGHT: A lyrical moment from the film. The film's many images of pure beauty counterpoint the world of spectacular horror it presents elsewhere. Anatoli Solonitsyn plays Rublev.

TOP RIGHT: The solitary Individual framed against a bleak landscape – Tarkovsky's own conception of the artist in society?

ANDREI RUBLEV

USSR 1966
DIRECTED BY
ANDREI TARKOVSKY

Screenplay:
*Andrei Mikhalkov Konchalovsky
and Andrei Tarkovsky*
Music: *Vyacheslav Ovchinnikov*
Photography: *Vadim Yusov*
185 mins

Leading players:
*Anatoli Solonitsyn, Ivan Lapikov,
Nikolai Grinko, Nikolai Burljaev.*

Andrei Rublev has had a history that is almost as tortured as its hero. Made in 1966, it was first shown at the 1969 Cannes Film Festival, much to the disapproval of the Russian delegation and cut by forty minutes (it nevertheless won the International Critics Prize). In an open letter to the Soviet newspapers in 1970, mainly in defence of the Nobel Prize awarded to Alexander Solzhenitsyn, the distinguished cellist and conductor Mstislav Rostropovich queried why his fellow citizens had not yet had the opportunity to see *Andrei Rublev*. It was finally released in Moscow in 1971, subject to some cuts agreed by Tarkovsky, and was more widely circulated in the West in 1972.

This seems a lot of fuss about a historical film. Rublev was a famous Russian icon painter of the fifteenth century. Tarkovsky's film is not a biography as such but a series of imaginative episodes from his life. These dramatize his inner conflict, which compels him towards silence and creative inactivity because he feels his art cannot help people. They also sketch a vivid picture of the brutality and desecration of the times.

It is a violent film (there is a horrific story that, for a shot of a cow in flames, Tarkovsky set fire to an animal himself). It is also visually imaginative, shot predominantly in black and white until a burst of colour towards the end celebrates the recognition of Rublev's work. Tarkovsky has always argued that his films should be felt emotionally rather than rationally, and approached as poetry more than narrative. Jean-Paul Sartre once described him as a 'socialist surrealist', which suggests not only the complexity of his work but implies the reason that it might be occasionally abhorrent to the Soviet authorities. In defiance of State insistence that Soviet films should be made for the masses, Tarkovsky's films are individualistic, esoteric works of an intensely private imagination, with a complex structure that challenges an audience's intelligence.

The official reason for the initial suppression of *Andrei Rublev* was, apparently, that the film gave a negative and indeed inaccurate view of history. One suspects that the really contentious area of the film was its philosophical and critical enquiry into the relationship between artist and society. *Andrei Rublev* concerns the struggle of a rebel artist against a society and authorities that seem hostile and obstructive. Given the furore over Shostakovich's Thirteenth Symphony (with its setting of Yevteshenko poems, which criticize Soviet anti-semitism) and Solzhenitsyn's outspoken novel *Cancer Ward*, there could hardly have been a more sensitive subject in the Soviet Union in the mid 1960s. For, although *Andrei Rublev* is a historical film, its modern relevance was not only apparent but deliberate. 'I do not understand historical films which have no relevance to the present,' says Tarkovsky. He has continued to make extremely original and arresting films, such as *Solaris* (1972) and *Stalker* (1979) which have further alienated him from the authorities. His recent defection to the West seems the inevitable consequence of his particular artistic sensibility.

115

WEEKEND

FRANCE 1967
DIRECTED BY
JEAN-LUC GODARD

Screenplay: *Jean-Luc Godard*
Music: *Antoine Duhamel*
Photography: *Raoul Coutard*
95 mins

Leading players:
Jean Yanne, Mireille Darc,
Jean-Pierre Leaud.

A critic once described a Jean-Luc Godard film as 'like a hand-grenade thrown amongst an audience'. *Weekend* is terrorist cinema, a work of assault and provocation directed at what Godard sees as the total exhaustion of modern Western civilization – social, cultural and political.

The basic situation is that of a weekend vacation for a wrangling middle-class couple that turns into a nightmare struggle for survival. They are forced off the road by a massive traffic jam, the tracking shot along which occupies seven minutes of screen time, involves a cross-section of seething humanity slowly bursting at the seams, and is accompanied by an incessant cacophony of car horns that seems an aural metaphor for social chaos. *Weekend* is a film about breakdown.

The married couple whose private reveries reveal dreams of pornography and murder and whose relationship culminates in cannibalism, represent Godard's view of the breakdown of the bourgeois family as the natural unit for ordering contemporary civilization. In stumbling across Emily Brontë in flames and a performance of a Mozart sonata in a barnyard, the couple are involuntary witnesses of the irrelevance of culture, which no longer seems a civilizing influence on the behaviour of man. (The further they go back to Nature, the more brutalized they become.) They are also confronted by political activists who lecture them about the crisis of capitalism, materialist exploitation and Third World politics. The film's alienation devices, such as captions and direct addresses to the audience, and its violent disruptions of cinematic illusion and narrative, are similar attempts to politicize the cinema,

freeing the spectator from passive enslavement into active engagement.

Eisenstein was the chronicler of the Revolution, Soviet-style: Godard is the cinema's spokesman for disaffected Western Man, anti-authoritarian, anti-American, anti-Imperialist, anti-bourgeois. Godard is perhaps the most formidable practising theorist and intellectual in the cinema since Eisenstein, less rigorous, more humorous. *Weekend* might be a Marxist deductive analysis on the garbage heap of Western civilization, but it is also suffused with the surreal logic of a Lewis Carroll, in which figures from literature, history and fantasy keep chuntering across each other's path without making contact. Godard's perception of the breakdown of social continuity accounts for the film's breakdown of narrative continuity. Could Godard belong any more to the bourgeois intellectual class whom *Weekend* excoriates as flat, devitalized and corrupt? Could he continue making such statements within an institution of cinema whose bland conservatism and frank commercialism embody the values he despises and rejects? *Weekend* was the moment when Godard, like James Joyce with *Finnegan's Wake*, went beyond the pale. From that point onwards, Godard has not attracted followers, fans or admirers: only disciples.

Opposite, top: The carnage of the car crash, which causes the traffic jam that will force the husband and his wife off the road, and which prophesies the breakdown of Western civilization. Bottom: Back to nature. Roland (Jean Yanne) and Corinne (Mireille Darc) take to the woods, a route that will confront them with their own bestiality. Above: Roland sits on top of a dustcart, listening, unconcerned, as an African and an Algerian deliver monologues on Third World exploitation and the necessity for violence against oppressors.
Right: Mozart in a barnyard. The odyssey of Roland and Corinne is interrupted when they are required to attend a concert, at which the pianist (Paul Gegauff) muses about the relevance of art to the world outside. Below: Roland and Corinne encounter a figure from history, one of several such interruptions as Godard seeks an explanation of the current state of Western civilization through reference to its cultural and political past.

A CLOCKWORK ORANGE

GB 1971

DIRECTED BY
STANLEY KUBRICK

Producer: *Stanley Kubrick*
Screenplay: *Stanley Kubrick*
Based on the novel by
Anthony Burgess
Music arranged by
Walter Carlos
Photography: *John Alcott*
Warner Brothers. 136 mins

Leading players:
Malcolm McDowell,
Patrick Magee, Anthony Sharp,
Adrienne Corri.

Although voted the best film of 1971 by the New York Film Critics, *A Clockwork Orange* almost immediately ran into a storm of controversy which, to this day, has not entirely abated. Some found it a 'film of major importance' and 'a brilliant piece of cinematic art'. Others called it 'hateful and contemptible' and accused it of 'sucking up to the thugs in the audience'. The film is certainly provocative, but is it socially irresponsible?

Based on Anthony Burgess's 1962 novel and set in the near future (1985?), the film continues the fascination with the application of science and man's primitive aggression that Stanley Kubrick had analysed in his previous film, *2001* (1968). The narrator and main character Alex (Malcolm McDowell) is an anti-social thug who preys on the old and infirm and gets his kicks from violence, such as a brutal attack on a liberal writer (Patrick Magee) and the rape of the writer's wife (Adrienne Corri). When arrested and imprisoned for murder, he submits to the Ludovico Treatment, whereby an aversion to sex and violence is instilled into him through a course of drugs. However, this scientific attempt to turn Alex into a model citizen is to have disastrous and far-reaching consequences.

The film is a thesis on the ambiguities of free will. It considers the proposition that a man who does not have the choice of being either good or evil is no longer human but a robot, a 'clockwork orange'. In order to allow the audience as far as possible to exercise its own free will, Kubrick makes the argument open-ended. Liberals and reactionaries are equally satirized. Alex is a monster (to sentimentalize him would be to obscure the moral point of the story, Kubrick thought), and seems a nightmare projection of the most destructively anarchic elements in man's subconscious. But he is also the only character with whom one could possibly sympathize.

Complicating the thesis even further is the film's complex, individual style. A battle between rival gangs is choreographed to the music of Rossini. Alex and his gang commit a hideous rape whilst also performing a parody of the Gene Kelly routine for 'Singin' in the Rain'. At such moments, an audience is transfixed with nervous tension, simultaneously amused by the incongruity and appalled by the inhumanity.

A Clockwork Orange is a futuristic black comedy with an Orwellian fear of political authoritarianism. Its world is deliberately grotesque and distorted, visually (the horrific distorting lens for the murder), verbally (the strange 'Nadsat' language of Alex) and musically (electronic Beethoven, to suggest the feeding into a warped mind of one of the great monuments of Western culture). The film is acted by McDowell, Magee and Anthony Sharp (as

the politician) in a vibrant horror-comic style. It is an explosive film, that might prove dangerous if it fell into the wrong hands, or minds. But, if one believes in the sovereignty of human choice, which is the film's main theme, then this is a risk that a liberal, civilized society should – and must – take.

TOP LEFT: Alex (Malcolm McDowell, rear, second from right) has a drink of moloko-plus with his mates in the Korova Milkbar.

FAR LEFT: Alex stands in the lobby of his contemporary flatblock, a typical uncared-for high rise, returning home after a typical evening of ultra-violence. *Inset*: Malcolm McDowell as Alex, who loves drugs, violence and Ludwig van Beethoven.

ABOVE: Alex asserts his leadership in the gang to Dim (Warren Clarke). George (James Marcus) looks on.

LEFT: The Lodovico Technique works. Alex's aversion therapy is successfully demonstrated to an excited press conference, as Alex finds himself nauseated by the demonstration model (Virginia Wetherell).

BELOW: Alex finds refuge in the house of one of his own victims, the writer (Patrick Magee, with his back to camera), after being beaten up by the police. He is carried in by the writer's bodyguard (Dave Prowse).

CRIME

Scarface (1932) · *White Heat* (1949) · *Bonnie and Clyde*
(1967) · *Chinatown* (1974)

Films about crime often provoke controversy, either because of their violence,
their sympathy for the criminal, or their criticism of society. Those considered
in the following pages are all controversial in these different ways – and
profoundly stimulating.
LEFT: The death of the gangster, Tony Camonte, in *Scarface*.
ABOVE: Bonnie Parker (Faye Dunaway) and Clyde Barrow (Warren Beatty)
posing for fame and notoriety in *Bonnie and Clyde*.

SCARFACE

USA 1932

DIRECTED BY
HOWARD HAWKS

Producers: *Howard Hughes and Howard Hawks*
Screenplay: *Ben Hecht*
Based on the novel by Armitage Trail
Music: *Adolph Tandler, Gus Arnheim*
Photography: *Lee Garmes*
United Artists. 90 mins

Leading players:
Paul Muni, Ann Dvorak, Boris Karloff, George Raft, Karen Morley, Osgood Perkins, Vince Barnett.

Scarface is subtitled 'Shame of a Nation' and has a prefatory statement on the credits declaring that it is 'an indictment of gang rule in America'. It is doubtful whether anyone has taken much notice: certainly the film itself does not. To judge by the success of films like *Little Caesar* (1930), *Public Enemy* (1931) and *Scarface*, it seems likely that the public saw movie gangsters not as 'the shame of the nation' but as daring opportunists taking advantage of a social system that did not work – which was the *real* shame of the nation.

Scarface is based on the career of Al Capone, although Howard Hawks's instruction to his writer Ben Hecht was 'to imagine it as the Borgias set down in Chicago'. It follows the rise and fall of Tony Camonte (Paul Muni), whose motto is: 'Do it first, do it yourself, and keep on doing it.' His progress follows the customary pattern whereby the gangster's growing power leads to increasing isolation and paranoia. Camonte is finally to be gunned down opposite a travel office which mockingly flashes the neon sign, 'The World is Yours'.

The critic Manny Farber described the people in *Scarface* as 'cavemen in quilted smoking jackets'. There is a primitiveness about their behaviour and outlook that the film exploits both for comic and serious purposes. The film makes fun of their incongruously underdeveloped response to civilization. One of them threatens a phone with a gun, and Camonte acknowledges the description of his place as 'gaudy' with the cheerful response: 'Isn't it, though? Glad you like it.' The disquieting moments come through their casual immaturity about violence, the sense of their actions as children's games played with deadly toys. There are fifteen murders in *Scarface*, often accompanied visually by images of flowers, which reinforce the perversity of the violence, or by images of the cross, which emphasize the profanity of violence. Two deaths are unforgettable: Camonte's murder of his coin-tossing henchman Guino (George Raft), the death signalled by the coin Guino habitually caught now falling to the ground; and the murder offscreen of a rival mobster (Boris Karloff) in a bowling alley, the camera following his last ball as it strikes the pins, which spin and fall over in a morbid metaphor for his death-throes.

'Whenever I hear a story,' Hawks said once, 'my first thought is to make it into a comedy, and I think of how to make it into a drama only as a last resort.' It might be the film's sheer impudence that allows it to get away with so much, including an unmistakably incestuous relationship between Camonte and his sister Cesca (Ann Dvorak). For all its moralizing interludes, it comes over as a black comedy about a public enemy's eccentric conception of private enterprise.

TOP LEFT: Camonte (Paul Muni) takes a childlike delight in his first machine gun. On his left are the ganster's moll, Poppy (Karen Morley) and the coin-tossing Guino Rinaldi (George Raft). The film's sense of comedy and play often catch an audience off guard when the violence comes and intensifies the sense of shock.
ABOVE: A rival gangster, Gaffney (Boris Karloff), who is to be shot by Camonte in a bowling alley.
TOP CENTRE: Camonte is about to supplant, and murder, his chief, Johnny Lovo (Osgood Perkins).

TOP RIGHT: Camonte's sister, Cesca (Ann Dvorak), is becoming attracted to Guino. They are to be married, but Camonte will murder Rinaldi in an incestuous rage.
ABOVE: Cesca intends to kill her brother for the murder of her husband, Guino.
RIGHT: Cesca changes her mind about revenge when the cops arrive, and brother and sister prepare to shoot it out, side by side.

WHITE HEAT

USA 1949
DIRECTED BY RAOUL WALSH

Producer: *Louis F. Edelman*
Screenplay: *Ivan Goff and*
and Ben Roberts
Suggested by a story by
Virginia Kellogg
Music: *Max Steiner*
Photography: *Sid Hickox*
Warner Brothers. 114 mins

Leading players:
James Cagney, Virginia Mayo,
Edmond O'Brien, Steve Cochran,
Margaret Wycherley.

The current of the times passes like a lightning rod through the action of *White Heat*. With his cry of 'Top of the World!', its manic hero evokes another megalomaniac whose attempted global domination provoked the Second World War. The mushroom cloud which concludes this work dramatically explodes the gangster film into the nuclear age.

During the 1930s, the gangster could still be portrayed as a tragic hero, either a victim of society or a dynamic if misguided individualist. In the immediate post-war era, the portrayal has been bloodied, darkened and de-romanticized. Richard Widmark's hoodlum in *Kiss of Death* (1947) is a giggling psychopath, whilst Edward G. Robinson's Johnny Rocco in *Key Largo* (1948) is a deluded dinosaur. The most extraordinary example of the trend is James Cagney's Cody Jarrett in *White Heat*. There is a continuity with the characters he played in the previous decade, particularly in *Public Enemy*; but now these drives have been twisted into murder and mania. Jarrett is a man with a 'red-hot buzzsaw inside my head', a one-man Wild Bunch raging for freedom in a dehumanized jungle. Jarrett's mother-love is not some revelation of his sentimental side, but the very essence of his psychological dementia.

It would be impossible to over-praise the daring with which Cagney carries off this performance. He is not afraid to risk looking ridiculous if it is the only route to sublimity. He sits on his mother's lap. He communes with his dead mother in the

woods and then defiantly, with menacingly hooded eyes, challenges his friend Fallon (actually a police informer) to find anything abnormal about his behaviour. Cagney knows he has the skill to control any possible absurdity and can chill the audience with a sudden glimpse of the abyss. Responding to Walsh's crackling direction and recurrent imagery of thunder, electricity and steam that reflect Jarrett's psychological storms, Cagney himself seems a ball of destructive energy. In the scene in the prison refectory where Jarrett learns that his mother is dead, Cagney takes us with complete conviction from stunned surprise to howling hysteria. Jarret's first reaction is to look down ('That first moment must be private, personal,' Cagney said, astutely): then you can practically hear his mind cracking.

Cagney's performance violently shakes the sympathies of the film. The original story was a hymn to the sophistication and efficiency of police technology, demonstrating crime detection advancing with science whilst the criminals remained anachronistic animals. But we watch Cagney's Cody Jarrett with appalled fascination whereas we can only view Edmond O'Brien's treacherous Fallon with disdain, as the ultimate Organization man who unblinkingly obeys orders. He is hardly the heroic alternative to Cody Jarrett, who is the American Dream – liberty and the individual – taken to a grotesque extreme. 'Made it, Ma! Top of the world!' he screams, before firing the bullet that will blow this world sky-high. He goes out trailing his own demented clouds of glory, the demons in his head finally exploding in an unresolved tension between self-affirmation and annihilation.

OPPOSITE, TOP: Cody Jarrett (James Cagney) and his mother (Margaret Wycherley) decide the fate of the wounded gang member, whose face has been scalded by a blast of steam during the train robbery. CENTRE: In the car, Jarrett and his mother discuss tactics, whilst Cody's sluttish wife, Verna (Virginia Mayo), looks on, excluded and disapproving. 'With you around, Ma,' Cody is to say, with disturbing devotion, 'nothing can stop me.' BOTTOM LEFT: Whilst Cody is in prison, Verna starts an affair with Big Ed (Steve Cochran). Big Ed is planning to take over the gang by arranging for an 'accident' to happen to Jarrett in prison. TOP RIGHT: Posing as a fellow prisoner, police informer, Hank Fallon (Edmond O'Brien), gains Jarrett's trust when he saves his life during a murder attempt in the prison workshop. RIGHT: 'Made it, Ma! Top of the world!' In the final shoot-out the mortally wounded Jarrett fires the bullet that will blow him and his world sky high.

BONNIE AND CLYDE

USA 1967
DIRECTED BY ARTHUR PENN

Producer: *Warren Beatty*
Screenplay: *David Newman and Robert Benton*
Music: *Charles Strouse*
'Foggy Mountain Breakdown' by Earl Flatts and Lester Scruggs
Photography: *Burnett Guffey*
Warner Brothers. 111 mins

Leading players:
Warren Beatty, Faye Dunaway, Michael J. Pollard, Gene Hackman, Estelle Parsons.

'A time creates its own myths and heroes,' said director Arthur Penn about his film *Bonnie and Clyde*. 'If the heroes are less than admirable, that is a clue to the times.' The real-life Bonnie Parker and Clyde Barrow might have been petty, vicious hoodlums but, to many reeling from the Depression in the 1930s, they were Robin Hoods striking a blow against the banks, the law and a society that had betrayed people's hopes. *Bonnie and Clyde* is about the split between the reality of Bonnie and Clyde and the legendary status thrust upon them, which they enjoy and foster but for which they are to pay a terrible price. The fact that the film had such an enormous impact on its release in 1967 has something to say about those times too.

Although set in the 1930s, the film is unlike the traditional gangster film, being rural and romantic and having a nervous savagery about its rhythm that is quite unlike the gangster film's usual terse, documentary-like economy. Depression America is evoked in a stylized way – peeling Roosevelt posters, desolate sites, decaying banks – to suggest a trance-like devitalized society that, by contrast, highlights the energy of the Barrow gang. The tone leaps wildly between comedy and shock, involving an audience with the gang's crazy exploits and then, with a violent slap, snapping that involvement back in an audience's face.

The film discomfited many contemporary critics, who accused it of social irresponsibility, romanticizing criminals, and encouraging violence. Bonnie and

Clyde are presented and were perceived as analogous to Sixties drop-outs, the Barrow gang forming their own hippie commune in defiance of authority. Their forays for fun, food and fame at the expense of a glum, discredited established order seemed to connect with a Sixties mood of youth protest at authoritarian hypocrisy – most potently symbolized by the Vietnam war.

But there are two stings in the tale of *Bonnie and Clyde*. The film is not a celebration of anarchy but an ironic, critical perception of the American propensity for violence. Penn sees this as rooted in the American frontier heritage, which modern civilization has moderated but not eradicated, and also in a sexual puritanism from which violence is sometimes the only release from repression. Bonnie and Clyde exemplify this, but, inevitably, they will also become the targets of it. Also the very success of the real-life Bonnie and Clyde (and the film *Bonnie and Clyde*) in mobilizing or antagonizing large sections of public opinion might encourage an over-reaction, both for and against. In the film, they become the victims of a blood-soaked backlash in which the forces of tradition will re-establish themselves with renewed righteousness. In retrospect, the convulsive and cataclysmic violence that concludes *Bonnie and Clyde*, the violence of the reactions to the film, seem prophetic of the traumatic events of 1968 that will tear the divisions in American society wide open – the assassinations of Robert Kennedy and Martin Luther King, the riots at the Democratic Convention, the election of President Nixon.

OPPOSITE, TOP: Clyde Barrow (Warren Beatty) teaches Bonnie Parker (Faye Dunaway) how to shoot.
CENTRE: Bonnie assists in the hold-up of a bank.
BOTTOM: Clyde takes a photograph of the Barrow gang. Bonnie poses by the car. Clyde's brother, Buck (Gene Hackman), holds his disapproving wife, Blanche (Estelle Parsons), whilst C. W. Moss (Michael J. Pollard) looks on. Photographs will be important in the film, for they will spread the fame and notoriety of the Barrow gang, making them publicized as well as public enemies.
TOP RIGHT: Clyde (Warren Beatty) in the cornfield. Bonnie has run off after the encounter with the undertaker: it is a portent of the blood-letting to come.
RIGHT: Bonnie is wounded as she, C. W. Moss and Clyde cross the river to escape from the surrounding police. The impact of the film's violence comes partly from the film's natural settings and partly from its colour. In previous gangster films, blood was usually black and white, not red.

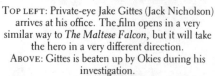

TOP LEFT: Private-eye Jake Gittes (Jack Nicholson) arrives at his office. The film opens in a very similar way to *The Maltese Falcon*, but it will take the hero in a very different direction.
ABOVE: Gittes is beaten up by Okies during his investigation.
ABOVE, RIGHT: Gittes is about to pay the penalty for poking his nose into Noah Cross's business. The psychopath wielding the knife is played by the film's director, Roman Polanski. 'Who's the midget?' asks Gittes, as he sees the menacing knifeman (Roman Polanski, *inset*) approaching.
OPPOSITE, TOP: Gittes has lunch with Noah Cross (John Huston), who seems deeply embroiled in the mystery. Gittes is to expose Cross's corruption, but will fatally underestimate his power.
BOTTOM: Gittes beats the awful truth out of Mrs Mulwray (Faye Dunaway) – that she has been raped by her father, Cross, and that her daughter is the incestuous product of that union.

CHINATOWN

USA 1974
DIRECTED BY
ROMAN POLANSKI

Producer: *Robert Evans*
Screenplay: *Robert Towne*
Music: *Jerry Goldsmith*
Photography: *John A. Alonzo*
Paramount. 131 mins

Leading players:
Jack Nicholson, Faye Dunaway,
John Huston.

The evil in *Chinatown* is twofold: property fraud on a massive scale (the film is a sour account of the formation of the city of Los Angeles), and brutal incest. As the writer Robert Towne summarized it: 'It is a story about a man who raped the land, and his daughter.' At the beginning, with its Thirties setting and its pleasingly intricate plot, the film evokes nostalgia for the private-eye genre. By the end, one is all but overwhelmed by the scale of the sexual and political corruption uncovered by a detective who had assumed he was investigating a case of marital infidelity.

Jack Nicholson, as the private-eye, and Faye Dunaway, as the feminine embodiment of mystery and danger, inhabit the Bogart–Bacall roles of old. But times have changed. Nicholson is not as smart as he thinks he is, and Dunaway's brittle wit is not a display of independence but a cover for neurosis. The humanity of the film comes through its revelation of the woman's anguish, and the transformation of the detective's cynical detachment into genuine horror. It is a nice touch to cast John Huston as Dunaway's monstrous father. It evokes *The Maltese Falcon*, which Huston directed, but is a reminder of the distance we have travelled from that world.

Chinatown has a very different kind of director, Roman Polanski, who pumps poisonous colour and savage violence into the formula. He has a small role himself as a knife-wielding psychopath, slashing Nicholson's nose as a warning to keep it out of other people's business. For the next hour, the private-eye has to wear a clumsy bandage over that nose. A comic detail perhaps, particularly when he wears it while entertaining Dunaway, and the band is heard to play 'The Way You Look Tonight'. But it is also a fearful reminder of his fallibility and the malevolence of the world in which he moves. He is finally to be revealed as a man out of his depth.

Chinatown is a calculated assault on the complacent certainties of the traditional detective film, in which good always triumphed and the individualist hero saw that justice was done. In *Chinatown*, the detective solves the crime, but that is all he solves. In the last scene in Chinatown itself (which throughout has accumulated associations of lawlessness and bad luck), he is defeated by the forces he sought to overthrow and destroys the people he sought to help. A shot is fired, a car horn blares out a fatal distress signal, and the detective turns numbly away from the human wreckage and is swallowed up in the dark streets.

Towne and Polanski had a fierce argument over that last scene, which Polanski won. He insisted on a pessimistic conclusion which he felt truthfully reflected the modern age. *Chinatown* shows the limit of individualism, the invincible conspiracies of power, and the irresistible allure of evil. When Nicholson asks Huston towards the end what all this corruption and murder has really been for, Huston replies: 'The future! The future!' It is a bloodchilling thought, and the film ensures that we take that thought seriously.

EPIC

Napoleon (1926) · *Seven Samurai* (1954) · *Ben-Hur* (1959) ·
Dr Zhivago (1965) · *War and Peace* (1964–7)

Epic films explore grand themes on a grand scale. Religion is the grand theme
of *Ben-Hur*. The sub-title of the novel by Lew Wallace reads: 'A Tale of the
Christ'.
LEFT: The Sermon on the Mount.
Revolution is the theme of *Dr Zhivago*. ABOVE: Zhivago is abducted by
guerrillas.

NAPOLEON

FRANCE 1926
DIRECTED BY ABEL GANCE

Screenplay: *Abel Gance*
Photography: *Jules Kruger*
305 mins

Leading players:
Albert Dieudonné,
Antonin Artaud,
Abel Gance, Annabella.

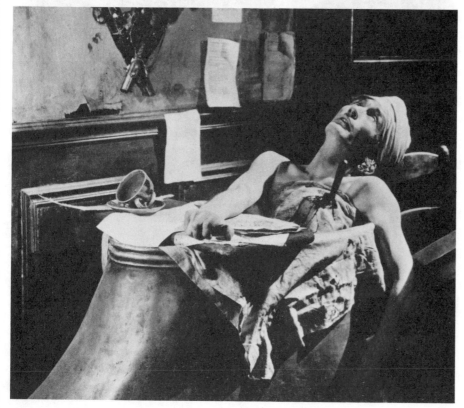

'The day of the Image has arrived,' declared director Abel Gance, for whom the cinema was not just a vocation but, in his own words, 'the climax of life'. *Napoleon* was intended as nothing less than a technical revolution. Following the innovations of epics such as Griffith's *Intolerance* and Stroheim's *Greed*, *Napoleon* unfortunately shared a similar fate to those films in seeming too ambitious for the cautious, conventional cinema of the day and being subjected to cuts or neglect. In recent years, however, thanks largely to the efforts of film historian Kevin Brownlow, a large part of *Napoleon* has been restored.

The film concentrates on the first half of Napoleon's life, from boyhood to his triumphant military campaign in Italy in 1796. Gance's conception of his hero's life is that of a man with an obsessive sense of destiny (symbolized in the film by an eagle) who is dragged towards war by a chain of circumstances he is unable to prevent. However, despite Dieudonné's compelling performance, in some ways the character does not seem to be the focus of the film. The star of *Napoleon* is the camera.

It is a film of stunning virtuosity and unparalleled camera fluidity. An opening snowball fight, in which Napoleon's precocious strategic cunning is already apparent, is filmed as if the camera were an actual participant. The film uses colour, superimposition, slow motion, split screen, sometimes also alluding to great art (as in the murder of Marat, which is posed as in David's famous painting). Gance fastens the camera to a cantering horse when he wishes to film a particularly

TOP LEFT: The young Bonaparte (Wladimir Roudenko), a pupil at the military college of Brienne.
CENTRE LEFT: The march into Italy begins – *Les Mendiants de la Gloire* (Beggars of Glory) follow Napoleon into history.
LEFT: The murder of Marat (Antonin Artaud), stabbed in his bath by Charlotte Corday. The composition recalls the painting by Jacques-Louis David.
RIGHT: Napoleon (Albert Dieudonné) bids a fond farewell to his wife, Josephine (Gina Manès) before joining his army.
RIGHT, ABOVE: The man of destiny; Napoleon on horseback.
FAR RIGHT: Failing to win Corsica for the Revolution, Napoleon is forced to run for his life, and he puts to sea in a small boat, watched by pursuing mounted gendarmerie. 'For me the cinema is not just pictures,' said Gance. 'It is something great, mysterious and sublime, for which one should not spare any effort and for which one should risk one's life if the need arises.'

hectic chase. During the extraordinary sequence where Napoleon is fighting a storm at sea whilst the Convention rages in Paris, Gance mounts the camera on a giant pendulum so that its swinging movement seems to plunge an audience into the very heart of these events and into the personal and political storms that are engulfing France in waves of revolution.

Gance's chief innovation was the introduction of Polyvision, a triple-screen process that anticipated Cinerama by a quarter of a century. 'The theme, the story one is telling, is on the central screen,' explained Gance. 'The story is prose, and the wings, the side screens, are poetry.' It was an awesome attempt to convey a visual synthesis of the physical, mental and emotional dimensions of an event. Only the film's final part is now available to be seen in this form (Gance destroyed other sequences in a fit of despair), and it gives some idea of its excitement. But it seemed too odd and expensive at the time. When sound came to the cinema a few months after the film's opening, *Napoleon*, which is dedicated to the absolute primacy of the image, looked even more of an anomaly. Gance never adjusted to talkies. His greatest pleasure in later life (he died in 1981) was the re-discovery of *Napoleon* by a new generation of astonished film-goers and film-makers.

SEVEN SAMURAI

JAPAN 1954
DIRECTED BY
AKIRA KUROSAWA

Screenplay: *Hideo Oguni,*
Shinobu Hashimoto and
Akira Kurosawa
Music: *Fumio Hayasaka*
Photography:
Asaichi Nakai Toho
200 mins

Leading players:
Toshiro Mifune, Takashi Shimura.

It has been a critical tradition to consider the great Japanese director, Akira Kurosawa, as 'an Oriental John Ford'. This would not displease Kurosawa: he is a great admirer of Ford. It is a description which draws attention to the direct appeal in the West of Kurosawa's work and the ease with which his films have been converted into Westerns. *Rashomon* (1950) was translated into a strange Hollywood opus, *The Outrage* (1964), with Paul Newman taking the role of the bandit that Toshiro Mifune had played in the original. *Yojimbo* (1961) was virtually plagiarized by Sergio Leone for the first of his spaghetti westerns with Clint Eastwood, *A Fistful of*

Dollars (1965), both offering a satirical and iconoclastic view of their traditionally noble heroes. Most famously, *The Magnificent Seven* (1961) was a skilful popularization of one of the great epics of Japanese film, *Seven Samurai*.

Many have imitated Kurosawa's plots; none has emulated his style. With its dynamic editing, its bold use of telephoto lens for sudden looming close-ups, its unexpected slow-motion for scenes of battle (long before this became a cinematic cliché), *Seven Samurai* is action cinema at its most artistic. When turning on the heat of his technical virtuosity, Kurosawa is one of the most stirring of modern film-makers.

The plot is simple. In the sixteenth century, a village is being annually raided by marauding bandits, and the people ask seven samurai for help in defending themselves. What follows is a fascinating duel of strategy and counter-strategy between bandits and samurai, culminating in a breathtakingly filmed battle to the finish, with swords, guns and horses' hooves flailing and thrashing through the rain and mud.

The job is successfully accomplished but, at the end, the samurai must leave the village, their violent skills having no place in the future life of the peasants. 'The samurai pass over the land like the wind,' says their leader, played with great dignity

by Takashi Shimura. 'But the land remains forever and the peasants forever with their land.'

Because of its length, its attention to historical detail and its location shooting, *Seven Samurai* was an expensive film to make and took a year to complete. At one stage the producers were getting cold feet and considering cancelling the whole thing. They telegraphed Kurosawa to return at once from his location. In reply, Kurosawa told them either to fire him immediately or leave him alone. They left him alone, to create a masterpiece. When it comes to individualist conviction, fearless integrity and dedication to a cause, Kurosawa has always been something of a samurai himself.

OPPOSITE, TOP: The villagers plant rice. 'The Samurai pass over the land like the wind. But the land remains forever and the peasants forever with their land.'
BOTTOM: The duel. The winner of this duel, the swordsman on the right, will be recruited to join the Samurai who are preparing to defend the peasants from marauding bandits.
LEFT: The Seven Samurai. Toshiro Mifune is prominent in the foreground, holding his sword. Takashi Shimura plays their leader (second from right).
BELOW: A close detail from the battle scene, as Mifune fearsomely thrashes a foe. This kind of detail, shot by Kurosawa using a telephoto lens, adds great impact and immediacy to the battle.
BOTTOM: The final battle, on rain-soaked land in inches of mud. Kurosawa has few rivals for conveying physical excitement on the screen.

BEN-HUR

USA 1959
DIRECTED BY
WILLIAM WYLER

Producer: *Sam Zimbalist*
Screenplay: *Karl Tunberg*
Based on the novel by
General Lew Wallace
Music: *Miklos Rozsa*
Photography: *Robert Surtees*
MGM. 217 mins

Leading players:
Charlton Heston, Jack Hawkins,
Stephen Boyd, Haya Harareet,
Hugh Griffith.

One of William Wyler's first jobs in the film industry was as an assistant on the silent version of *Ben-Hur* (1926), helping to organize the extras in the arena for the filming of the chariot race. Thirty years on, the remake of *Ben-Hur* was to win Wyler his third directing Oscar (after *Mrs Miniver* and *The Best Years of Our Lives*).

Although there were a number of fine Hollywood epics made during this period (*Spartacus, Barabbas, El Cid*), *Ben-Hur* remains the greatest of them. This is not simply because of the technical splendour of the action scenes, like the sea battle and the ferociously exciting chariot race. The film has an unusually fine script. Quite apart from Karl Tunberg's credited contribution, which composes dialogue exchanges in a discreet and beautiful blank verse, the poet and playwright Christopher Fry also supplied deft phrases to give an appropriate sense of period. Gore Vidal worked on the relationship between the former boyhood friends, the Jewish nobleman Ben-Hur (Charlton Heston) and the Roman commander Messala (Stephen Boyd), planting an implication that Messala's brutality against the hero and his family springs from a feeling of unrequited love. Certainly Boyd's performance was the finest, most passionate of his career.

Wyler never sacrifices psychology for spectacle. For him, *Ben-Hur* was a story about the struggle of the Jews for their freedom, a theme which he thought an urgent and still topical issue. Also, as films such as *Friendly Persuasion* (1956) and *The Big Country* (1958) indicated, Wyler was particularly preoccupied at this time with the themes of pacifism and revenge, and these are at the heart of *Ben-Hur*.

Portrayed with true epic dignity by Charlton Heston, Ben-Hur is a divided man, searching for identity in a world of conflicting faiths and alternate grandeur and barbarity. These divisions are intensified when his best friend Messala becomes his worst enemy, forcing him into the role of victimized Jew; and when his fiercest foe, the Roman commander Quintus Arrius (Jack Hawkins) becomes his keenest patron, forcing Ben-Hur now into the role of triumphant Roman. Through this tortured character, the film pursues the morality of revenge, as the hero gradually is in danger of becoming the very thing he set out to destroy. The conflicting claims on Ben-Hur of Messala (who has tried to kill him) and Christ (who

has given him water in the desert, and so saved his life) pulls the film between extremes of violence and repose that are shadowed by an equally extreme visual surface – formal and stately in the untroubled opening, agitated and restless in the convulsive finale. The conclusion appropriately emphasizes the purification of the innocent rather than the punishment of the guilty, and parallels Ben-Hur's relinquishing of vengeance in favour of forgiveness.

It would be hard to overpraise the film's skill in sustaining character and structure amidst the potential diffuseness of the epic form. With expert supporting performances and a stupendous Miklos Rozsa score, *Ben-Hur* is a moving, intelligent epic from a rare director who knew that popularity and profundity need not be contradictory aims.

OPPOSITE, TOP: A scene from the 1926 version of *Ben-Hur*, after the sea battle with the pirates. Ramon Novarro (Ben-Hur) and Frank Currier (Arrius) are in the boat.

CENTRE: 'No water for him!' says the Roman sentry. But he is defied by Christ who gives water to Ben-Hur (Charlton Heston) on the way to his slavery in the galleys.

ABOVE: The reunion of the childhood friends, Messala (Stephen Boyd), and Ben-Hur (Charlton Heston), shortly to become bitter enemies.

TOP: After they have been rescued from the raft Arrius (Jack Hawkins) offers water and friendship to Ben-Hur. Note the use of the water imagery: the water, proffered first by Christ, now by Arrius, symbolizes two alternative paths of life that are being offered to Ben-Hur. It recurs in the scene after the Crucifixion.

RIGHT: The chariot race in which Ben-Hur rides for vengeance and national pride against his Roman enemy, Messala.

Dr Zhivago

USA 1965
Directed by David Lean

Producer: *Carlo Ponti*
Screenplay: *Robert Bolt*
Based on the novel by
Boris Pasternak
Music: *Maurice Jarre*
Photography: *Frederick Young*
MGM. 197 mins

Leading players:
*Omar Sharif, Julie Christie,
Rod Steiger, Alec Guinness,
Tom Courtenay, Geraldine Chaplin,
Ralph Richardson, Klaus Kinski,
Rita Tushingham.*

Banned in the Soviet Union but acclaimed in the West, Boris Pasternak's Nobel-Prize winning novel, *Dr Zhivago* is a great love story and a great documentary of the Russian Revolution. The controversy surrounding the novel in its own country probably stems from its passionate advocacy of the importance of the personal life. Between *Potemkin* and Pasternak, there is a wholly different artistic and political spirit. *Potemkin* is about the way in which collective action embodies the spirit of the Revolution; *Zhivago* is about the contribution of the Revolutionary experience towards the maturing of a great Russian poet, Zhivago, who is a surrogate of Pasternak himself.

Working again with his screenwriter from *Lawrence of Arabia*, Robert Bolt, David Lean fashions an epic canvas in which characters' lives are swept off their expected paths by the arbitrary and often cruel winds of history. The film could be described as a fateful series of brief encounters. From the moment when an attempted killing disrupts the plush politeness of a Christmas Eve party, the fates of the four main characters become inextricably wedded: the lovers Zhivago and Lara, who are seeking a haven of peace and poetry in a world that will not let them rest; the sensual opportunist Komarovsky, who is trying to keep his feet in a society of slippery political allegiances; and the student Pasha whom brutal suffering is to transform into the ruthless revolutionary Strelnikov.

The complicated narrative is held together by a series of connecting, associative images: moon, windows, candles; cornflowers and daffodils to suggest the two women in Zhivago's life; the tram on which Zhivago is casually to spot Lara for the first time (sparks immediately fly) and years later, heartbreakingly, for the last time; the recurrent train journeys, carrying the loved ones either to or from each other, and which suggest a whole society in transit. Intense emotional moments are conveyed in imagery that interlocks the political and personal stories: the cut from the blood on the white snow after the Cossack massacre to a close-up of Lara after losing her virginity to Komarovsky; the shot of the smouldering candle through a frosty window pane, on the inside Pasha and Lara in furious argument, on the outside the light spotted by Zhivago as he passes, unaware of the way his whole life will be changed by these two people. Lean throughout enriches the emotional and thematic texture through expressive use of Nature, that can terrify and inspire, that can rejuvenate and kill.

Of the performances, the most memorable impressions are those of Julie Christie's sensuous warmth as Lara, Rod Steiger's truly Dostoevskian demonism as Komarovsky, and Alec Guinness's alternate sternness and subtlety as Zhivago's half-brother. More than the performers, it is the splendour of groupings, spectacle, David Lean's directorial eye, that one remembers. There is a stunning last shot of Lara, as she disappears alone down a grey street that is dominated by a huge red poster of Stalin. It is an image that crystallizes the theme of the individual and the State, as well as implicitly asking questions that are at the heart of *Dr Zhivago* – what the Revolution was for, where it led, and, above all, whom it affected.

OPPOSITE, TOP: The Cossacks break up a peaceful march, spattering the snow with blood.
BOTTOM: Marching off to war in 1914.
CENTRE: Komarovsky (Rod Steiger) rapes Lara (Julie Christie). This scene of personal violation is crosscut with the political violence of the Cossacks taking place nearby.
ABOVE: The family arrive in Siberia, but finding their house boarded up, take refuge in the cottage. Zhivago's wife, Tanya (Geraldine Chaplin), carries their son. Zhivago (Omar Sharif) is in the centre; his uncle (Sir Ralph Richardson) is on the right.
LEFT: The student Pasha who has now become the revolutionary, Strelnikov (Tom Courtenay), aboard his train. 'Revolution erupted forcibly like a breath held too long,' says the novel. 'Everyone seemed to experience two upheavals, his own personal revolution, and a second one, common to all.'
BELOW: After he has escaped from his captors, Zhivago crosses the frozen wastes in search of his family.

TOP LEFT: Ludmilla Savelyevia made her screen debut as Natasha.
ABOVE: At the ball.
LEFT: The September hunt sequence. Natasha is on horseback.
BOTTOM LEFT: The duel in the snow. Pierre (Sergei Bondarchuk, right) about to fire.
BELOW: Pierre, the conscience of the whole story, and played with impressive authority by the film's director, Sergei Bondarchuk.
TOP RIGHT: A commander watches the advance of his drummers and prisoners, with the peasants cowering nearby. A good example of the film's spectacular wide-screen compositions in depth.
BOTTOM RIGHT: The cannon is brought into action during the ferocious fighting.

WAR AND PEACE

USSR 1964–7
DIRECTED BY
SERGEI BONDARCHUK

Screenplay: *Sergei Bondarchuk
and Vasily Solovyov*
Based on the novel by Leo Tolstoy
Music: *Vyacheslav Ovchinnikov*
Photography: *Anatoly Petritsky*
Mosfilm. 507 mins (Russian version,
released in four parts: English
version 357 mins, released in
two parts).

Leading players:
*Ludmilla Savelyevia,
Sergei Bondarchuk,
Vyacheslav Tikhonov,
Vasily Lanovoi, Irina Skobotseva,
Boris Zakhava,
Vladislav Strzhelčhik.*

The greatness of Tolstoy's epic novel, *War and Peace*, E. M. Forster thought, came not so much from its plot or people but from its symphonic sense of space, which seemed to correspond to the immensity of Russia itself. 'After one has read it for a bit,' Forster said, 'great chords begin to sound . . . they come from the immense area of Russia, over which episodes and characters have been scattered, from the sum-total of bridges and frozen rivers, forests, roads, gardens, fields, which accumulate grandeur and sonority after we have passed them.'

It is this sense of physical massiveness – of visual space more than narrative length – that the Russian film above all captures. In this respect, it is interesting to compare it with King Vidor's 1956 adaptation of the novel. Vidor's Natasha (Audrey Hepburn) conveys an inner growth and maturity much more surely than Bondarchuk's heroine, whose acting inexperience is exposed in her failure to capture the important development of the character. On the other hand, Pierre, who is the conscience and voice of humanity of both films, is much more successfully realized in the Soviet film, Bondarchuk seeming sensitive and authentic beside Henry Fonda's uncomfortable performance in the Vidor. But it is in its response to nature and in its sense of the scale of battle that the Russian film really scores. Its majestic autumnal landscapes or scenes such as the September wolf hunt have an exhilaration and pathos that dwarfs the American version by comparison. This is not simply spectacle for its own sake but a recognition of something crucial in the novel: a feeling for the wonder and imperishability of Nature which cuts the arrogant, ephemeral political ambitions of a Napoleon down to size. True to the spirit of Tolstoy, the film depicts war as a sordid reality that can nevertheless produce individual gestures of beautiful heroism. Its extensive recreation of the battle of Borodino is one of the great spectacles of modern cinema.

Four years in the making and enormously expensive, *War and Peace* was a phenomenal success in Russia. According to one source at the time, Soviet statistics suggested that there wasn't an

adult in the country who had not seen it. On the strength of it, Bondarchuk was to make another massive film on a similar theme, *Waterloo*, with Rod Steiger as Napoleon. But this was to prove much less successful.

In one of his last interviews before his death in 1910, Tolstoy talked about the potential of the cinema and the challenge it represented to the old methods of literary art. He was excited by the new medium. He liked it for its swift changes of scene, its capacity for instantly blending emotion and experience, its mastery of the mystery of motion, and its life-like ability to convey the hurricane force of human feeling. For all these reasons, he would surely have liked the film of *War and Peace*.

LEFT: A panoramic view of the Tsar's army as it marches into battle.
TOP: Napoleon (Vladislav Strzhelchik) follows the progress of the French advance at Borodino.
ABOVE: The people retreat from Moscow as Napoleon's army advances into the city.

SOCIAL REALISM

The Crowd (1929) · *The Grapes of Wrath* (1940)
The Best Years of Our Lives (1946) · *Bicycle Thieves* ·
On the Waterfront (1954)

As well as being a medium for mass entertainment, the cinema has often sought to reflect and comment on the real world. Some of the greatest films have been made about the problems of ordinary people, appealing to audiences through showing them a heightened reflection of their own lives.
LEFT: Father (Lamberto Maggiorani) and son (Enzo Staiola) in *Bicycle Thieves*.
ABOVE: Husband (James Murray) and wife (Eleanor Boardman) in *The Crowd*.

THE CROWD

USA 1928
DIRECTED BY KING VIDOR

Producer: *Irving G. Thalberg*
Screenplay: *King Vidor,*
John Weaver, Harry Behn
Photography: *Henry Sharp*
MGM. 113 mins

Leading players:
James Murray, Eleanor Boardman.

TOP: A confident Johnny Sims (James Murray) takes Mary (Eleanor Boardman) to Coney Island and tells her of his ambitions for the future before proposing marriage.

ABOVE: A domestic row between Johnny and Mary. In the heat of the moment, Mary forgets to tell him that she is pregnant: she has to call him back with the news.

ABOVE RIGHT: The parents stare in horror as they see their daughter in the street run over by a truck.

RIGHT: Johnny has started drinking and Mary is preparing to leave him.

OPPOSITE, TOP: Johnny loses his job. In its analysis of the effect of poverty and unemployment on the relationship between a father and his children, the film greatly influenced *Bicycle Thieves*.

FAR RIGHT: Made frantic by the city noises which he feels are disturbing the rest of his dying daughter, Johnny rushes into the street to try and silence the din. The people sweep past him, impervious. 'The world can't stop just because your baby's ill,' he is told by a passing cop.

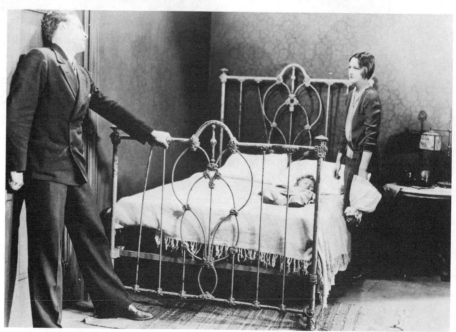

When King Vidor asked Irving Thalberg if the studio would support an offbeat project like *The Crowd* (a good question considering what had happened to Stroheim's *Greed*), Thalberg replied: 'MGM can afford a few experimental projects.' The originality of *The Crowd* lies in the essential simplicity of its idea. It is the story of an ordinary man in modern society. In bold defiance of screen convention of the time, the film follows the random pattern of life, without the insertion of melodramatic events, or the usually happy ending. Equally boldly, it offers a bleak picture of American society immediately before the Wall Street crash and a sour overview of the American Dream as seen from the vantage point of an average American.

Born at the turn of the century, the hero of *The Crowd* seems imbued with the optimism and potential of a new age. But his father's untimely death foreshadows his future disillusionment, a famous staircase shot of the boy seeming to isolate him in a void of foreboding between the innocence of the past and the menace of what is to come. He lands a job as a clerk, marries, raises a family, but his ambitions always outweigh his accomplishments,

and the twists of life seem to fuel his bitterness. When his daughter dies – the death presaged by a harrowing moment when he unavailingly tries to silence a crowd making a noise outside the sick child's window – his world falls apart. He loses his job and contemplates suicide.

It was not only the outspoken theme that marked *The Crowd* as an exceptional achievement for its time. The film's technique is as bold as its realism, with some remarkable location work in New York and an astonishing moment when, in what seems one continuous shot, the camera tilts up a skyscraper and gradually isolates the hero at his desk in a densely populated office. The performances of James Murray and Eleanor Boardman convey the cumulative pain of a disintegrating marriage with a restraint and psychological subtlety rare in silent screen acting. With tragic irony, Murray's career was to follow a similar path to that of his character in *The Crowd*, unable to capitalize on his big break, descending into self-destructive alcoholism that culminated in death by drowning in the Hudson River.

The film remains uncompromising to the end. Father takes his family to a show

and they laugh at the clowning, but are then seen as part of an audience similarly laughing at the tawdry entertainment – an image of conformity and adjustment in grim contrast to the exceptional career envisaged by the hero at the outset. Recently triumphantly revived at the National Film Theatre in London, with a new score by Carl Davis, *The Crowd* is one silent film which it would be difficult to surpass in a new version for the sound era. When exhorted by financiers to 'make films about the people', Jean-Luc Godard retorted tartly: '*The Crowd* has already been made – why remake it?'

USA 1940
DIRECTED BY JOHN FORD

Producer: *Darryl F. Zanuck*
Screenplay: *Nunally Johnson*
Based on the novel by
John Steinbeck
Music: *Alfred Newman*
Photography: *Gregg Toland*
20th-Century Fox. 129 mins

Leading players:
*Henry Fonda, Jane Darwell,
John Carradine.*

Are Hollywood and realism compatible? When Darryl Zanuck bought the rights of John Steinbeck's novel, *The Grapes of Wrath* in the late 1930s, many feared for the worst. Steinbeck's novel is both social document and socialist polemic, a tirade against the economic exploitation of migratory farm workers in California. How could that be reconciled with Hollywood's pursuit of happiness? In the event, the film has endured as securely as the book.

'The whole thing appealed to me, being about simple people,' said director John Ford. 'And the story was similar to the famine in Ireland when they threw the people off the land and left them wandering on the roads to starve.' The story is of the Joad family who are forced to leave their home in the dust-bowl of Oklahoma to seek a new life in California, only to find a situation even worse than the one they left – families billeted in labour camps and compelled to work for desperately low wages.

With cameraman Gregg Toland, Ford creates some unforgettable imagery of harsh sunlight and deep shadow. A farmer (John Qualen) squats near the ground, the eviction order in one hand, a piece of dirt in the other, his shadow reflected on the land in front of him. When his home is destroyed by a caterpillar tractor, the camera pans from a shot of the family to that of their shadows in front of them, as if the tractor has flattened *them* – as, in a way, it has. Equally memorable is the small moment of Ma Joad (Jane Darwell)

as she first cherishes, then burns, her mementoes before setting off for California; and the shot, from the Joads' point of view, as they enter the transit camp for the first time and are appalled by the poverty and squalor. Violence erupts and families are disrupted because of the terrible conditions. Eventually Tom (Henry Fonda) and Casey (John Carradine) are involved in a murderous anti-labour brawl and Tom, after avenging Casey's murder in a moment of passionate fury, is wanted by the police. Ma and her son must part, in a whispered farewell scene in the dark. 'Whenever there's a fight so hungry people can eat, I'll be there . . .' says Tom. Fonda invests the speech – and his whole performance – with the kind of controlled anger and fervour born out of a man's outrage at injustice. In a career of extraor-

dinary excellence, he did nothing nobler.

Over the years the film has been criticized for sentimentality, notably because of Ma's speech in the last scene: 'We're the people that live. They can't wipe us out, they can't lick us.' Ford's treatment of the material is humanist more than political. For him the tragedy lies in the destruction of family rather than in governmental insensitivity. Any affirmative feeling in the film comes not through communal politics, as in the novel, but from a sense of human indomitability. Steinbeck's radical realism and Ford's poetic lyricism are very different, but in *The Grapes of Wrath* seem, magically, to arrive at the same theme from a different route. That theme has been stated by a character in the novel: 'All that lives is sacred.'

OPPOSITE, TOP: Muley (John Qualen) relates the destruction of the homesteads by the 'cats' to Tom Joad (Henry Fonda) and Casey (John Carradine).
CENTRE: Tom Joad and the family load up the ramshackle truck with their belongings to head for California.
BOTTOM: Grandmother (Zeffie Tilbury) has died but Ma Joad (Jane Darwell) tells the patrolman that grandmother is only 'very sick', so that they will be allowed to continue their journey. If Tom expresses the anger of the film, Ma Joad will express its heart.
BELOW: The Joads look out towards California. Will it prove to be the promised land?
BOTTOM LEFT: Tom tells Ma and Pa Joad (Russell Simpson) of his dismay at the appalling conditions in the transit camp.
BOTTOM RIGHT: John Carradine as Casey, who tries to organize opposition to the exploitation of the working families in the labour camps.

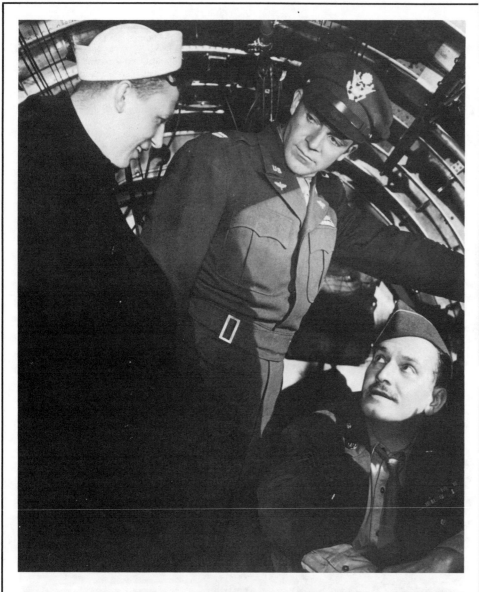

THE BEST YEARS OF OUR LIVES

USA 1946
DIRECTED BY
WILLIAM WYLER

Producer: *Samuel Goldwyn*
Screenplay: *Robert Sherwood*
Based on the novel *Glory for Me*
by Mackinlay Kentor
Music: *Hugo Friedhofer*
Photography: *Gregg Toland*
RKO. 172 mins

Leading players:
*Fredric March, Myrna Loy,
Teresa Wright, Dana Andrews,
Virginia Mayo, Cathy O'Donnell,
Harold Russell.*

The realism of *The Best Years of Our Lives* stems from its unforced humanity, its observation of ordinary people whom one comes to care about, and its seemingly transparent style. Gregg Toland's magnificent deep-focus photography, which permits background and foreground detail to be simultaneously visible in the frame, allows the drama to unfold naturally before one's eyes. In William Wyler's view, this method is more 'democratic' than montage, allowing an audience

OPPOSITE, TOP: Three ex-servicemen, Homer (Harold Russell, left), Fred (Dana Andrews, centre) and Al (Frederic March) meet on the plane taking them home after World War II.
BOTTOM: Al gets drunk on his first night home. He is watched by Fred and Al's wife, Milly (Myrna Loy) and gently restrained by Homer and the bar's pianist, Butch (Hoagy Carmichael).
FAR LEFT: Fred's marriage to Marie (Virginia Mayo) is beginning to disintegrate. 'I gave up the best years of my life,' she says angrily, about their marriage.
LEFT: A drugstore customer (Ray Teal, on the floor) has been flattened by Fred after haranguing Homer, who attacks him for questioning whether the war sacrifice was worthwhile.
BELOW: Peggy (Teresa Wright) shocks her parents by declaring her love for Fred and her determination to win him away from his wife. Notice the drink in her father's hand. Al's drinking problem is to grow subtly worse during the film.

greater freedom to do its own editing of detail. One way or another, 'democracy' is a key theme of the film.

The film concerns the difficulties of readjustment to civilian life of three servicemen returning to America after World War II. Al (Fredric March) returns to an influential banking position, but finds it difficult to reconcile old loyalties with new commercial realities. Fred (Dana Andrews) cannot hold down a job or pick up the threads of his marriage. Having had both hands burnt off during the war, Homer (real-life amputee, Harold Russell) cannot convince himself that his fiancée's feelings are still those of love and not pity. The lives of the three occasionally intersect, and all are reunited at Homer's wedding. When the marriage vows are exchanged, the camera permits us to see simultaneously three couples for each of whom these words have a quite different meaning – joyous, bitter and ironical. It is a good example of the concise suggestiveness of Wyler and Toland's method.

It is a happy ending of sorts, but the essential irony of the film's title remains. The film is about men who have given the 'best years of their lives' to fight for freedom, as have the women in their sustaining stability at home. The question the film asks is: does the post-war America they find indicate that their sacrifice was worthwhile? Photographs around the house seem to recall a happier and now irretrievable past. The film's visual claus-

trophobia emphasizes the rough scramble for jobs and the danger of certain people being elbowed aside. 'Last year it was kill Japs, this year it's make money,' says Al. The film's precarious optimism about their readjustment is weighed against marital and class strains and a new spirit of rampant commercialism.

There are some particularly memorable set-pieces: Al's return home; Fred's exorcizing war-time ghosts in an airplane graveyard; the celebrated moment where, as Al watches Homer improvise on a piano, Fred in the phone booth at the back

is breaking off his relationship with Al's daughter – a virtuoso sequence in which every inch of the screen is being used for expressive effect. The performances are splendid (Fredric March, in particular, has never been finer). Its popularity and success (it won seven Oscars) perhaps obscured the courage of its social criticism and its air of disquiet. Wyler imparts his characteristic dramatic sense and meticulous craftsmanship to material to which, with his own war experience and clear-sighted attitude to America, he felt he could bring particular conviction.

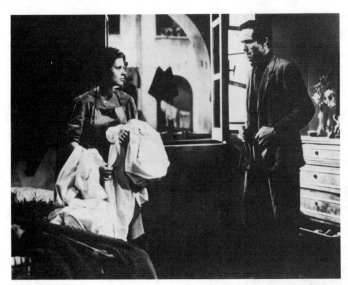

BICYCLE THIEVES

ITALY 1948
DIRECTED BY
VITTORIO DE SICA

Producer: *Umberto Scarpelli*
Screenplay: *Cesare Zavattini*
Based on the novel by
Luigi Bartolini
Music: *Alessandro Cicognini*
Photography: *Carlo Montuori*
90 mins

Leading players:
Lamberto Maggiorani,
Enzo Staiola.

Within three years of its international release, *Bicycle Thieves* had been voted best film ever made by a poll of leading critics circularized by the magazine, *Sight and Sound*. Yet the film had been made on a tiny budget, with a cast of non-actors, and with a subject so slight that it would scarcely raise a headline in a newspaper (a

OPPOSITE, TOP LEFT: Antonio Ricci (Lamberto Maggiorani) and his wife Maria (Lianella Carell) prepare to pawn their sheets to raise some money.
TOP RIGHT: Having obtained a job as a billposter, Antonio collects his bicycle from the pawnshop.
CENTRE: As he puts up a poster, Antonio turns in horror to see a thief pedalling away on his bicycle.
BOTTOM LEFT: Antonio and his son Bruno (Enzo Staiola) sit disconsolately on the curb, their spirits almost crushed.
BOTTOM RIGHT: Searching in the rain. The weather seems to correlate to the hero's gathering despair.
ABOVE: Antonio confronts the man whom he is convinced is the thief. However, the thief is to have an epileptic fit and be protected by friends. Antonio must retreat, frustrated.
RIGHT: In desperation, Antonio tries to steal a bicycle himself outside a sports stadium and is immediately caught. Bruno watches in anguish.
The cycle owner will decide not to prosecute, reading Antonio's cruel predicament from his face.

bill-poster's livelihood is threatened when his bicycle is stolen). How can one account for its esteem?

Initially, one should remember the period in which it appeared. It seemed to represent a healthy reaction against Italian film melodrama and romance of the war years, and to Hollywood escapism. It brought ordinary people on to the screen, not only exposing post-war poverty but seeming to rediscover the film camera's own unique capacity as an instrument of social observation. *Bicycle Thieves* is informed by a passionate anger at social conditions that reduce people to desperate measures.

The film also cleverly combines the illusion of reality with the structure and emotional power of art. It is a tightly constructed work, whose basic narrative is a tense alternation between search and chase, as the bill-poster seems first to find and then lose the thief. As he and his son cross the city in search, a whole host of social detail is uncovered – the clutter at the pawnshop, the dispassionate union meeting, the gloomy church service, the exploitative fortune teller, the brothel. The observation seems spontaneous and peripheral, but each of these institutions is offering itself as a relief from suffering in a desperate human situation, and the film is equally critical of them for their glib panaceas.

Simultaneously the film is exploring the relationship between father and son. The father's character is to disintegrate under the pressure of events, to the point where he attempts to steal a bicycle himself. By observing this through the eyes of a child, the film gives added emphasis to the man's loss of dignity, whilst highlighting the innocent child's premature awareness of social cruelty and injustice. Yet the enduring bond between father and son is the most positive humanity glowing through the film.

Nowadays it is more common for critics to be sceptical about the film's limited political analysis. Even in its time, it was attacked by the Right, in its own country, for its unflattering picture of Italy, and by the Left for compassionate defeatism and a brand of realism that seemed to induce despair more than revolt. But *Bicycle Thieves* is aimed at the emotions and its depiction of the ravages of unemployment in the mode of drama-documentary nowadays seems more relevant than ever. It seeks not to explain the political reasons for poverty but to make an audience feel for poverty's victims, whose humiliation and desperation force them, tragically, to steal from each other in order to survive. Its unobtrusive technique gives the illusion of an unmediated window on the world. Here is a film, one feels, that is telling the truth.

ON THE WATERFRONT

USA 1954
DIRECTED BY ELIA KAZAN

Producer: *Sam Spiegel*
Screenplay: *Budd Schulberg*
Based on articles by
Malcolm Johnson
Music: *Leonard Bernstein*
Photography: *Boris Kaufman*
Columbia. 108 mins

Leading players:
Marlon Brando,
Eva Marie Saint, Karl Malden,
Lee J. Cobb, Rod Steiger.

A vivid depiction of corruption on the New York dockland, *On the Waterfront* could be described as 'polemical realism'. It packs a punch. Its detestation of tyranny and intimidation has the fervour of an Eisenstein, but the message is fundamentally American: a hymn to individualism.

The individual is an ex-boxer, Terry Malloy (Marlon Brando), torn between his instinctive sense of justice and loyalty to his brother Charlie (Rod Steiger), who is the gangsters' lawyer. His feelings are complicated further when he falls in love with the sister (Eva Marie Saint) of a man whom he has set up for murder. He confesses this to the girl, the tension emphasized by the sound of a clangorous dockland drill which serves as an emotional correlative to the girl's sense of shock and the clanking chaos inside Terry's head. Charlie tries to straighten Terry out (a famous scene in the back of a cab, with Brando and Steiger at their best), but seems only to awaken Terry's dormant disillusionment. When Charlie is murdered by the gangsters, Terry testifies against them on the witness stand.

On the Waterfront is one of the most ambitious of gangster films, its realism emphasized by its unusually close observation of a working-class community. The location shooting adds to the authenticity: this is one film one could not imagine in a studio. The film has much carefully wrought imagery (like the murdered boy's jacket, which becomes a mantle of danger, conscience and possibly death, to whoever wears it, or the pigeons that Terry tends, which suggest his lurking tenderness), but it is integrated naturally into the action. The film's raw sense of conviction comes mostly from the performances, in which every role seems not so much acted as inhabited.

On the Waterfront was the third screen collaboration of one of the American cinema's greatest actor/director combinations, Marlon Brando and Elia Kazan (they had previously worked together on *A Streetcar Named Desire* and *Viva Zapata*). Brando's performance is Method Acting at its finest, feeling a character from the inside and, with an eloquent array of gesture, hesitation, expression, vocal inflection, conveying the man's inarticulate inner confusion. Kazan's direction has that edge of visual aggression and rhetoric that marks his most vibrant films. In this film, he had something to prove.

After his testimony, Terry is beaten up by the gang but, bloodied and unbowed, leads the men back to work. If this conversion of Brando's anti-hero into noble martyr seems surprising and inflated, one should consider the context in which the film was made. During the investigations of the House of UnAmerican Activities Committee, Kazan confessed his former membership of the Communist party and 'named names' of other members to the Committee. The ennoblement of Terry's act of conscience could be Kazan's own act of self-justification. With its groping towards self-respect and political optimism, *On the Waterfront* is a cauldron of personal anguish and public humiliation, whose qualities and complexes make it an invaluable document of the time.

FAR LEFT: Waterfront boss Johnny Friendly (Lee J. Cobb) displays his scars to ex-boxer Terry Malloy (Marlon Brando). Terry is showing remorse at the murder of a man who was planning to testify against Friendly. Friendly insists that Terry's concern is misplaced.
LEFT: Terry falls in love with Edie Doyle (Eva Marie Saint), sister of the man Terry has set up for murder.
BELOW: Terry and Edie flee down a darkened street from a truck. The driver intends to kill them.
RIGHT: One of the great scenes of American cinema. In the back of a taxi-cab, Terry's lawyer brother, Charley (Rod Steiger), tries to persuade Terry not to testify to the Crime Commission. Their argument will lead to Terry's bitter recriminations against his brother. 'I could've had class,' Terry insists, 'I could've been a contender.'
BOTTOM: Encouraged by Father Barry (Karl Malden), Terry, although badly beaten up by Friendly and his henchmen, leads the men back to work.

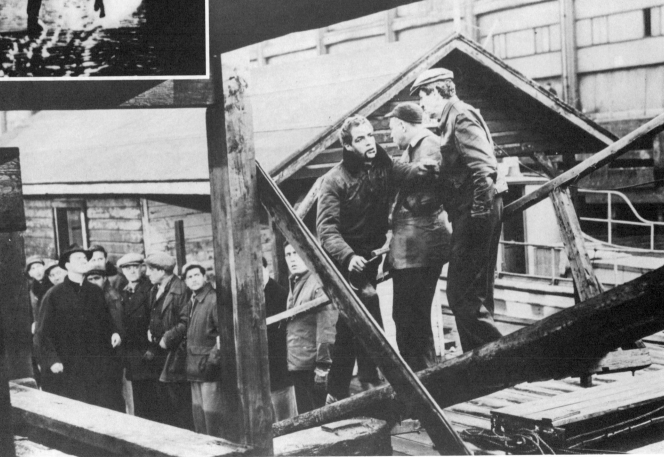

THRILLERS

The Maltese Falcon (1941) · *The Third Man* (1949) ·
North By Northwest (1959) · *Klute* (1971) · *Jaws* (1975)

'The suspense is terrible,' said Oscar Wilde, 'I hope it will last.' The thrillers in
this section have all lasted splendidly.
LEFT: The search for Harry Lime in the sewers of Vienna in *The Third Man*.
ABOVE: Peter Lorre holds up Humphrey Bogart in *The Maltese Falcon*.

THE MALTESE FALCON

USA 1941
DIRECTED BY JOHN HUSTON

Producer: *Hal B. Wallis*
Screenplay: *John Huston*
Based on the novel by
Dashiell Hammett
Music: *Adolph Deutsch*
Photography: *Arthur Edeson*
Warner Brothers. 100 mins

Leading players:
*Humphrey Bogart, Mary Astor
Sydney Greenstreet, Peter Lorre,
Elisha Cook Jr, Lee Patrick,
Jerome Cowan.*

'It has rhyme and rhythm and makes the mind ask questions.' So said Raymond Chandler about the title of Dashiell Hammett's novel, *The Maltese Falcon*, and the description could apply to this film. Although the story had been filmed twice before, debutant director John Huston stuck much more closely to the text, was blessed with singularly fortunate casting, and fashioned a slick film mystery that is also a pungent study of selfishness and duplicity.

The eponymous black bird is a statuette of inestimable value. In pursuit of it are a dubious femme fatale Brigid O'Shaughnessy (Mary Astor), whose delicacy is spiked with venom; a nervous homosexual Joel Cairo (Peter Lorre), with a scented calling card in one pocket and a gun in the other; and a fleshy gentleman villain, Caspar Gutman (Sydney Greenstreet) whose bulk expresses the hugeness of his ego and the grossness of his greed. Drawn into the pursuit is private-eye Sam Spade (Humphrey Bogart), who has been hired by the girl on an ostensibly innocent assignment that has led to the murder of his partner.

The action of the film is mainly interior and the suspense comes not from physical danger but from the possibilities for psychological deception. Almost everything is seen from Spade's viewpoint. The brisk, unfussy visuals reflect Spade's own slick self-confidence and his ironical, somewhat superior attitude to human

frailty. However, there are limits even to his cynicism in a treacherous world, particularly in those moments when he explains the ethical code by which he must turn the girl over to the police. Bogart's performance is at its best here, the strain on his face reflecting Spade's tension between professional righteousness ('When a man's partner is killed, you're supposed to do something about it') and betrayal of a woman he loves.

Bogart and Huston were to collaborate on a number of films which gave Bogart some of his finest parts and where the element of adventure is inseparable from a form of psychological quest. *The Treasure of the Sierra Madre* (1947) explores the potential for paraonoia behind Bogart's tough-guy image, just as *The African Queen* (1951) reveals its potential for a gentle humanity.

For John Huston, *The Maltese Falcon* set the standard for what has proved one of the most offbeat of Hollywood careers. His literary sensibility, his love of eccentric characterization, his fascination for what he calls 'all left-handed forms of human endeavour' are all in this first film. *Falcon* is an amorality play about a group of charming but deadly liars, gripped by an obsession which, on the point of achievement, is to blow up in their faces. The falcon is 'the stuff that dreams are made of', as Spade says, but the sounds we remember are the resounding barks of Gutman's hollow laughter on discovering his precious bird is a fake. From *Falcon*, through *Sierra Madre* to *The Man Who Would Be King* (1975) Huston has mischievously specialized in perverse stories about life's capacity for scattering men's deepest dreams to the wind.

OPPOSITE, TOP: A mysterious woman, calling herself Miss Wonderly (Mary Astor) spins a tale about her missing sister to sceptical private-eye Sam Spade (Humphrey Bogart). Spade's partner, Miles (Jerome Cowan), eyes Miss Wonderly enchanted. Spade's investigation will begin in earnest when Miles, following up the woman's story, is murdered.
CENTRE: Bleeding from the head, Joel Cairo (Peter Lorre) has to be protected by the police (Barton MacLane, left, and Ward Bond, right) from the venom of the deadly female, now calling herself Brigid O'Shaughnessy. Spade watches, amused.
BOTTOM: Spade meets Gutman's gunsel, Wilmer (Elisha Cook Jr), who will later be sacrificed in Gutman's pursuit of the falcon.
LEFT: Spade has been drugged by Gutman (Sydney Greenstreet). Wilmer and Cairo look down, impassively.
BELOW: 'It's lead! It's lead! It's a fake!' Gutman's murderous quest for the falcon has ended in failure and disappointment. He is watched by Spade, Cairo and Brigid. Strangely, out of an exemplary cast, Greenstreet's performance was the only one to receive an Oscar nomination.

THE THIRD MAN

GB 1949
DIRECTED BY CAROL REED

Producer: *Carol Reed*
Original story and screenplay by
Graham Greene
Music: *Anton Karas*
Photography: *Robert Krasker*
London Films. 104 mins

Leading players:
Joseph Cotten, Alida Valli,
Orson Welles, Trevor Howard,
Bernard Lee.

Producer David Selznick held the American rights to this film, and thus had right of consultation over the final script. As well as proposing Noël Coward for the role of Harry Lime, Selznick was apprehensive about the title. 'Who the hell is going to go to a film called *The Third Man*?' he enquired.

In fact, even in a post-war period notable for vintage British cinema from artists such as Olivier, Powell and Pressburger, and David Lean, *The Third Man* proved to be special. Much of it is now enshrined in movie mythology: the mocking lyricism of Anton Karas's zither music; the setting of a devastated post-war Vienna that seems to mirror the decadence of some of the survivors; and a masterful autumnal final shot which might be subtitled 'the long goodbye' (and which represents the final crushing of the hero's illusions). Of the performances, Orson Welles is unforgettable as the saturnine yet ruthless Harry Lime.

At the beginning, Lime is presumed dead. His friend Holly Martins (Joseph Cotten) is suspicious of the circumstances of the death, but his investigations reveal not that Lime has been murdered but that he is a murderer, stealing penicillin, diluting it, and then selling it to unsuspecting patients. As the simple Martins – the innocent American in Europe – plunges farther into this world of nocturnal treachery, the sense of evil seems to spread like the contaminated penicillin with which Lime has made his money. Carol Reed's frequent employment of

distorted camera angles turns the world awry. Lime has finally to be rooted out of his hiding place in Vienna's sewers, which Graham Greene described as 'this strange world, unknown to most of us, that lies under our feet'. The exposure of Lime has similarly revealed to Martins depths of human depravity he never suspected.

Like Greene and Reed's previous collaboration *The Fallen Idol* (1947), *The Third Man* is a stark encounter between innocence and evil. It is also a study of betrayed friendships. Holly's idealized childhood memory of Harry is destroyed by the corruption he finds, whilst Harry is ignobly led into a trap by Holly. The casting of Joseph Cotten and Orson Welles has echoes of *Citizen Kane*, with Cotten once again playing the envious friend who

despises yet admires his colleague's disreputable daring.

Lime's amoral cynicism is a convincing legacy from a genocidal war. 'Would you really feel any pity,' he says to Holly on the Great Wheel, as they look down on the people below, 'if one of those dots stopped moving for ever . . ? In these days, old man, nobody thinks in terms of human beings. Governments don't, so why should we?' Lime's self-justifying pay-off line, about the irrelevance of morality, and apparently improvised by Welles on the spot, is unforgettable. Even the most barbarous ages produced great art, he says, whereas, 'in Switzerland they had brotherly love, five hundred years of democracy and peace, and what did they produce? The cuckoo clock! So long Holly.'

OPPOSITE, TOP LEFT: Looking into the mysterious death of his friend, Harry Lime, Holly Martins (Joseph Cotten) meets Harry's girl friend, Anna (Alida Valli), who is an actress at the Josefstadt Theatre in Vienna.
BOTTOM LEFT: Sergeant Paine (Bernard Lee) and Major Calloway (Trevor Howard) have discovered irregularities in Anna's papers and are taking her away for questioning.
LEFT: With the Great Wheel of Vienna in the background, Holly waits for Harry Lime. Lime is very much alive and Holly now knows him to be an international racketeer.
TOP: Orson Welles as Harry Lime trying to escape through the sewers of Vienna.
CENTRE: The manhunt in the sewers.
RIGHT: The final shot. Harry Lime has been buried, and Holly Martins (Joseph Cotten) now waits for Anna (Alida Valli), with whom he has fallen in love. Without a word, she will walk right past him and into the distance.

North By Northwest

USA 1959

Directed by
Alfred Hitchcock

Producer: *Alfred Hitchcock*
Screenplay: *Ernest Lehman*
Music: *Bernard Herrmann*
Photography: *Robert Burks*
MGM. 136 mins

Leading players:
*Cary Grant, Eva Marie Saint,
James Mason, Leo G. Carroll,
Jessie Royce Landis,
Martin Landau.*

'I am but mad north-north-west,' said Shakespeare's Hamlet. Hitchcock's Hamlet in *North by Northwest* is a smug advertising man, Roger O. Thornhill (the O, he says, stands for 'nothing'), who is suddenly thrust into a mad drama in which he is the leading actor but knows neither the plot nor the script. Sauntering into a hotel lobby (whose music at this juncture is, 'It's a most unusual day'), he is mistaken for a secret agent, and hustled along into a bizarre series of events that transport him from kidnapping in Madison Avenue through murder at the United

Nations to involuntary mountaineering on Mount Rushmore.

Nothing delights Hitchcock more than the ordinary man in an extraordinary situation, and the plot here seems to inspire him and his splendid writer Ernest Lehman to the most ingeniously outrageous invention. Thornhill is simultaneously pursued by the police for a murder he never committed, and by foreign spies for secrets he does not have. Force-fed with neat bourbon and dumped behind the wheel of a car, he then has to suffer the indignity of being charged with drunken driving after some hair-raising escapes from death. Directed to a spot of lonely countryside by a beautiful blonde he seems to have wooed on a train, he is suddenly sprayed with bullets by a low-flying biplane – a brilliant sequence that displays Hitchcock's relish for flouting screen convention and staging his darkest deeds in bright sunlight. Attacks from the air are to recur in one of his most powerful allegories, *The Birds* (1963), just as Thornhill's last supreme test of clinging for his life to the stone-faced Presidents of Mount Rushmore recalls the dizzying torment of the disturbed protagonist of *Vertigo* (1958).

In fact, lurking in the wings of *North by Northwest* are some tantalisingly serious themes, notably the plight of the average man at the mercy of ruthless governments (for, basically, Thornhill is being unwittingly used as a tool of the CIA). With their eruptions of chaos into a world of order,

and with sexual relationships that often develop into tense battlegrounds of deception and desire, Hitchcock's films never encourage complacency and have a unique capacity to disturb. But with Cary Grant on top form, splendidly supported by Eva Marie Saint's smouldering agent and James Mason's suave saboteur, the tension is preserved with the lightest of touches. As well as being a master of suspence, Hitchcock was known as an inveterate practical joker. *North by Northwest* is, cinematically, his most thrillingly sustained practical joke, perhaps the definitive example of what the Master meant when he described the cinema as 'not a slice of life, but a slice of cake'.

TOP LEFT: Murder at the United Nations. Roger Thornhill (Cary Grant) discovers a knife in the back of the ambassador (Philip Ober) and, by his action, implicates himself in the murder.
TOP: Thornhill is interrogated for secrets he does not possess by the suave Philip Vandamm (James Mason) and Vandamm's sinister assistant, Leonard (Martin Landau). The unusual high-angle shot seems to anticipate the aerial threats that will become a major part of Thornhill's experience in the film.
TOP RIGHT: Lured out to a deserted highway, Thornhill is chased by a biplane which has been spraying crops 'where there ain't no crops' and now sprays bullets at him.
CENTRE: Eve Kendall (Eva Marie Saint) pretends to shoot Thornhill in order to convince Vandamm of her loyalty to him and divert suspicion from the fact that she is a secret agent of the American government.
RIGHT: Thornhill and Eve attempt to escape from Vandamm's men across the stony face of Mount Rushmore.

KLUTE

USA 1971
DIRECTED BY ALAN J. PAKULA

Producer: *Alan J. Pakula*
Screenplay: *Andy K. Lewis and Dave Lewis*
Music: *Michael Small*
Photography: *Gordon Willis*
Warner. 114 mins.

Leading players:
Jane Fonda, Donald Sutherland, Roy Scheider, Charles Cioffi.

'I'm afraid of the dark,' says call-girl Bree Daniels (Jane Fonda) at one stage to private-eye Klute (Donald Sutherland), who has been spying on her while investigating the disappearance of a friend. Fear of the dark is the central theme of *Klute*. It is not only the fear of something that can strike without warning under the cover of night. It is also a fear of the darkness within the human personality itself, the potential for bestiality lurking unsuspected inside an ostensibly normal person which, in a certain set of circumstances, might suddenly explode into violence. *Klute* is a thriller that is not simply about crime: it is about Original Sin.

Although the film recalls famous 1940s private-eye classics such as *The Maltese Falcon* and *The Big Sleep* (1946), there are significant differences. The romanticism of the conventional form has gone, and some of its unacknowledged implications have been brought out into the open. The femme fatale is now explicitly a whore: the private-eye is now explicitly a voyeur. Klute has none of the repartee of the usual detective, and his investigation becomes a form of self-investigation. He rescues damsels in distress, but he is also enthralled and seduced by them. Klute's innocence stems from his being a country hick rather than a streetwise urban man. This might insulate him from the city's corruption: alternatively, it might make him more susceptible to it. Donald Sutherland's masterfully restrained performance makes Klute himself one of the film's biggest mysteries.

'What interested me about *Klute*,' said director Alan Pakula, 'was making a contemporary exploration through the slant of a classic form.' His contemporary exploration reveals alarming neuroses and paranoia. Modern communications, like the phone or the tape recorder, are terrifying, and the city is a Hell that projects a complete disharmony between the individual and his surroundings. The call-girl needs a psychiatrist, and the murderer is isolated in a sheer glass tower block that reflects his own alienation.

When the murderer comes to silence Bree, Pakula constructs an overhead shot to show the beast ascending in the lift out of a pool of darkness, just as the impulse to murder itself has surfaced from his subconscious.

The film's most original stroke is in its characterization of Bree, struggling for control and survival in a harsh world in which women are cosseted, exploited or abused. Her emotional attraction to Klute frightens her, because she feels it threatens her independence. Her alternating moods

reveal the tensions of the modern liberated woman whose quest for self-fulfilment demands alternative solutions to the traditional ones of love, marriage and motherhood. The ending is chillingly ambiguous. She is going away with the enigmatic Klute, but for how long, and to what? Will Klute himself turn out to be the darkness she fears? Perhaps because of her association with the Feminist Movement, Jane Fonda seems to understand this woman completely, and her moving performance is one of the dramatic highlights of contemporary cinema. It deservedly won her an Oscar.

LEFT: Private investigator, John Klute (Donald Sutherland, right), has come to New York to investigate the disappearance of Klute's best friend, who seems to have been leading a double life. With the aid of a call-girl, Bree Daniels (Jane Fonda), Klute begins asking around.
BOTTOM LEFT: High on drugs, Bree escapes from her growing emotional involvement with Klute by seeking comfort in the company of her sleazy pimp (Roy Scheider).
TOP RIGHT: Farther into the underworld. Klute and Bree visit a friend of Bree's, who might be able to help. The friend nervously waits for a drugs consignment to be delivered to her; the visit of Klute and Bree is unwelcome.
BELOW: Hearing footsteps on the rooftop of Bree's apartment block, Klute goes up to investigate.
BOTTOM RIGHT: 'You play on the sexual fantasies of men like me.' Bree struggles for survival with the murderer, Cable (Charles Cioffi), who has followed her and is now planning to kill her.

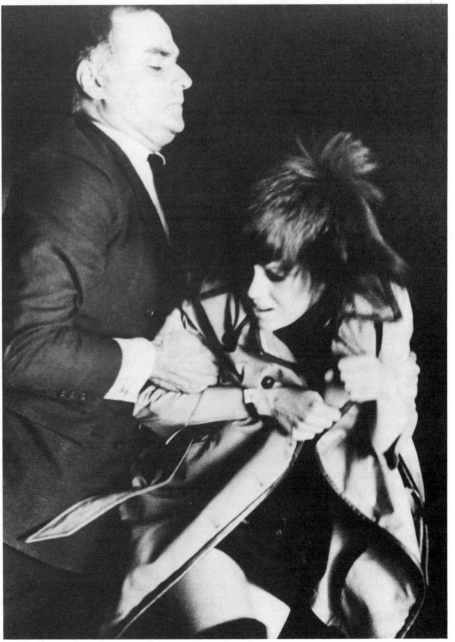

JAWS

USA 1975

DIRECTED BY
STEVEN SPIELBERG

Producers: *Richard D. Zanuck and David Brown*
Screenplay: *Peter Benchley and Carl Gottlieb.*
Based on the novel by
Peter Benchley
Music: *John Williams*
Photography: *Bill Butler*
Universal. 125 mins

Leading players:
Roy Scheider, Robert Shaw, Richard Dreyfuss.

Not since *Psycho* had a film offered such pleasurable terror as *Jaws*, doing for sharks what the Hitchcock film had done for showers. The film became a prototype of movie as event and of the new cinema of visceral sensation that drew a massive audience back to the cinema.

A shark is terrorizing the beaches of Amity, a resort that relies on tourists for its prosperity. For a long time the menace is not seen, only the grisly effect of its attacks on the victims. By concealing the shark but being able to suggest its presence through restless underwater camerawork and John Williams's sinister music, Spielberg can pull a few surprises and get round

the technical problem of visualizing the shark. Visual horror is frightening, but invisible horror adds a new dimension of terror. The shark's ability to sneak up unawares (often at moments of humour or repose) shatters human complacency and implies a malign intelligence on the part of the beast. The best scenes are those in which nothing happens, but where there is the suspense of expectation (like the scene of the Sheriff on the beach, his eyes fixed on the water and unable to concentrate on any conversation around him; or the moment when the shark, for the first time, rises from the water, fear given shape and dimension).

The film's popularity possibly stemmed from its expert balance between anxiety and reassurance. The shark never kills anybody sympathetic. Indeed its devouring greed is not that different from Amity: for some time, the Mayor conceals knowledge of the danger for fear of discouraging the tourist trade. Audiences might have linked this 'hushing up' of inconvenient truths with the recent Watergate scandal that had unseated President Nixon. Having evoked the atmosphere of Watergate America through its allusion to an unacknowledged menace under the surface of things, the film then sets about restoring communal confidence by bringing this menace to the surface and annihilating it.

Jaws develops into an elemental adventure yarn, alluding to practically every male maritime fantasy, from *The Ancient Mariner* through *Moby Dick* to *Three Men in a Boat*. The hunters are an obsessed sea captain (Robert Shaw) who has his own

score to settle with the shark; an ichthyologist (Richard Dreyfuss) who brings a modern technical expertise to the task; and the Sheriff (Roy Scheider) who hates the sea but is there out of civic duty. In the personality conflicts that follow, age is contrasted with youth, the man of the sea with the man of the city, and a macho assertion of primitive masculinity against the more modest aspirations of modern urban man. Like Hitchcock, Spielberg knows the value of humour in suspense, the way it can catch audiences off guard, relieve unbearable tension. *Jaws* is a most artful suspense construction. It may criticize the shark's consumerism and Amity's commercialism, but the film itself is a triumph of uninhibited consumerist packaging. As one critic put it, 'a shark of a movie'.

TOP LEFT: The Mayor (Murray Hamilton, left) is not amused by the defaced poster which could threaten the tourist trade of Amity. Sheriff Brody (Roy Scheider, centre) and the shark expert, Hooper (Richard Dreyfuss, right) try to convince him of the danger.
RIGHT: The terror begins: a female bather (Cindy Grover) is attacked by the unseen shark. 'The shark dictated all the shots,' said Spielberg.
OPPOSITE, TOP: Three men in a boat. Quint (Robert Shaw), Brody and Hooper try to tackle the shark. *Inset:* Robert Shaw as the ancient mariner, Quint, one of the few survivors of the shark attack on the shipwrecked *Indianapolis*. He is obsessed by sharks and seems gnawed by a premonition of his own death.
RIGHT: Brody watches from the safety of the boat as Hooper searches underwater for the missing seaman.
FAR RIGHT: The shark sneaks up unawares to attack Hooper in his underwater cage.

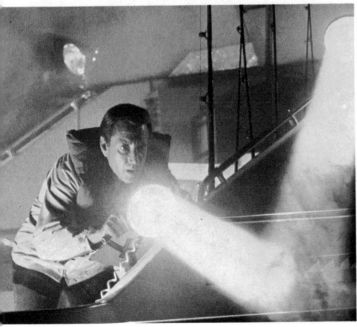

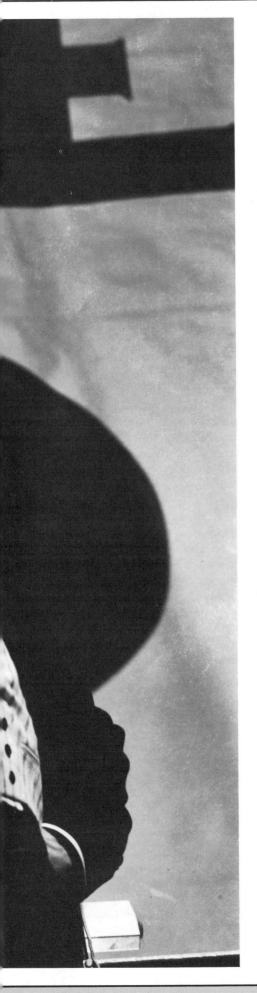

THE ART OF THE CINEMA

La Règle du Jeu (1939) · *Citizen Kane* (1941) · *Rashomon* (1950)
Sunset Boulevard (1950) · *The Apu Trilogy* (1955–8)
L'Avventura (1960) 8½ (1963) · *Persona* (1966)

Film is the art-form of the twentieth century. The following films are
masterpieces, made by directors who have used the cinema to express a
profound and personal view of life.
ABOVE: The gamekeeper (Gaston Modot) and his dog in *La Règle du Jeu*.
LEFT: Charles Foster Kane (Orson Welles) on the campaign trail in
Citizen Kane.

LA RÈGLE DU JEU
(The Rules of the Game)

FRANCE 1939
DIRECTED BY JEAN RENOIR

Producer: *Jean Renoir*
Screenplay: *Jean Renoir*
Musical Arrangements:
*Robert Desormieres and
Joseph Kosma*
Photography: *Jean Bachelet*
113 mins

Leading players:
*Marcel Dalio, Nora Gregor,
Roland Toutain, Jean Renoir,
Gaston Modot.*

Like good wine, *La Règle du Jeu* has matured with age. When it first appeared, audiences were hostile, distributors nervous, and even Renoir himself felt his own part (as Octave, the film's maladroit mischief-maker) ought to be trimmed. Nowadays, particularly after the restoration of a complete version in 1965, this film is generally regarded as a masterpiece. In 1939, people perhaps felt that it did not have the immediate nobility of theme of Renoir's previous film, *La Grande Illusion* (1937). More likely the hostility was a symptom of the sensitivity of the times, with the film's social portraiture being seen as, in Renoir's word, 'demoralizing'.

Ostensibly, *La Règle du Jeu* is about a house-party that goes wrong. The infidelities taking place above and below stairs become violently entangled. The two men ultimately victimized – an aviator (Roland Toutain), who is a guest at the party and in love with the hostess, and a gamekeeper (Gaston Modot), made ferociously jealous by his wife's flirtation – are the two who do not observe the rules. The correct form for emotional dealings in this society seems to consist of hypocrisy, insincerity, infidelity and absence of feeling. The aviator and the gamekeeper are doomed, because they feel deeply and do not take life and love as a game. As such, they are dangerous, because they threaten to tear down the façade of polite society to reveal the moral corruption beneath.

Two splendid set-pieces crystallize the film's themes and bring matters to a head. A shooting party forces the tensions between the characters out into the open. The horrific slaughter of the animals ('Hunting is a sport I detest, I consider it an abominable exercise in cruelty,' said Renoir) anticipates a tragic shooting which will conclude the theatrical entertainment and sexual sports in the evening, and the slaughter is also a prophecy of forthcoming battlefields in the theatre of war. The fancy dress ball in the evening becomes a *danse macabre* and a chilling metaphor for the artificiality of these people, their compulsive role-playing, and their assumption of masks in order to indulge raw desire rather than real feeling.

'It is a war film and yet there is no reference to the war,' Renoir said. 'Be-neath its seemingly innocuous appearance, the story attacks the very structure of our society.' Far from being a frivolous film, *La Règle du Jeu* is a ferocious attack on frivolity, an unnerving revelation of the spiritual fragility of the French ruling class. Renoir was holding up a mirror to the decadent condition of French society on the eve of a European war. If the French did not like what they saw, the reason might not be that they were affronted by it but were frightened by it. The criticism still has that generosity towards humanity that is so typical of Renoir, yet, in *La Règle du Jeu*, it is a generosity that is not without its own ambiguity, sadness and foreboding. 'The awful thing about this world, you know,' says Octave, 'is that everybody has his reasons.'

TOP LEFT: Octave (Jean Renoir) and the maid, Lisette (Paulette Dubost).
ABOVE: As the guests gather at the country house, the aviator André (Roland Toutain) converses with the Marquis (Marcel Dalio). The aviator is in love with the Marquis's wife, Christine, and has come to the weekend hunting party at the instigation of the Marquis's friend, Octave.
OPPOSITE, TOP RIGHT: At the shoot Christine spies her husband with one of their friends, Geneviève (Mila Parély). They have been having an affair but, unknown to Christine, her husband is at this moment ending his liaison with Geneviève.
FAR RIGHT: A deceptively cheerful conversation between Christine (Nora Grégor, left) and her husband's mistress, Geneviève.
CENTRE RIGHT: Marceau, the poacher (Julien Carette), is given employment by the Marquis, despite the objections of the gamekeeper, Schumacher.
RIGHT: In the kitchens the tension grows between Schumacher (Gaston Modot) and Marceau, particularly as Schumacher suspects Marceau of 'poaching' his wife, Lisette.

CITIZEN KANE

USA 1941
DIRECTED BY ORSON WELLES

Producer: *Orson Welles*
Screenplay:
Herman J. Mankiewicz,
Orson Welles
Music: *Bernard Herrmann*
Photography: *Gregg Toland*
RKO. 119 mins

Leading players:
Orson Welles, Joseph Cotten,
Dorothy Comingore,
Everett Sloane,
Agnes Moorehead.

If your first film is a masterpiece like *Citizen Kane*, there is one overriding problem: the future might be an anti-climax. Ironically, this parallels the theme of the film. Charles Foster Kane inherits a fortune: for the rest of his life, he is puzzling what to do with it.

Kane is a quintessentially American hero. One could say that he stands for some of the potentialities and contradictions of America itself. (The working title was 'American'.) He can be dynamic but also dangerous, confident but callous. He has the instincts of a democrat but the arrogance of an imperialist. He is a champion of the common man who ultimately becomes isolated as an Emperor in his own domain. He wants to be

OPPOSITE, TOP LEFT: Thatcher (George Coulouris) shakes hands with the boy Kane (Buddy Swan) who is clutching his 'Rosebud' sled. Father (Harry Shannon) and mother (Agnes Moorehead) watch anxiously.
TOP RIGHT: Kane outlines his plans for the *Inquirer* to Thatcher.
BOTTOM: Kane and his close friend, Jedediah Leland (Joseph Cotten), stand amongst copies of the *Inquirer*.
ABOVE: Kane, with his friends Bernstein (Everett Sloane) and Leland, celebrates his acquisition of top journalists from the rival newspaper, the *Chronicle*.
LEFT: Kane and his first wife, Emily (Ruth Warwick), the niece of the President. 'Say, before he's through, she'll be a President's wife!' says Bernstein.

loved, but on his terms, and, in general, he is a man who owns everything but possesses nothing.

Kane's life is investigated by a reporter. He consults the diaries of Kane's banker, who loathed him. He interviews Kane's business manager, who idolized him; his best friend, who deserted him; his second wife, who left him; and his butler, who patronized him. Each presents a different picture according to his or her particular perspective, so that the truth might be in the sum of what is said or somewhere else entirely. The reporter's main clue to Kane's character is the word he uttered on his death-bed: 'Rosebud'. Maybe this is the missing piece of the puzzle: it gives a focus to his search. The reporter never discovers its meaning: but we do, seeing 'Rosebud' inscribed on Kane's childhood sled as it is being consigned to the flames along with his other possessions. Perhaps 'Rosebud' symbolizes Kane's yearning after his lost innocence and carefree childhood, yet the flames consume the evidence almost before it registers and the mystery essentially remains.

Citizen Kane is a film of echo and shadow, dominated by a gigantic but hollow man whose life trails into a shadow of what it might have become. Kane is always making 'promises', but the promises remain unfulfilled, just like his own promise. The writer Borges described *Citizen Kane* as a 'labyrinth without a centre'. This is true both of Kane, who

remains an enigma even to himself, and of the film, which does seem to explain less the more it shows and is an extraordinarily sophisticated demonstration of the ambiguity of the visual world.

It is a film designed to amaze, with a nonchalantly complicated narrative structure, a sensationally imaginative soundtrack (from boldly overlapping dialogue to Herrmann's exceptional score) and total technical mastery, from Gregg Toland's stunning photography down to make-up

that conveys the ageing process with complete conviction. The film remains forever fresh, as if infused with the youth and audacity of its flamboyant creators, most of whom were new to the cinema. When Orson Welles was asked if he knew at the time he was making an important film, he replied: 'I never doubted it for a single instant.' Time has proved him right. *Citizen Kane* remains the Great American Film against which all other contenders must be measured.

OPPOSITE, TOP: A confrontation on the staircase with Kane's political rival, Gettys (Ray Collins), who is threatening to blackmail Kane over his affair with Susan (Dorothy Comingore). Emily watches anxiously.
BOTTOM: Susan's disastrous debut as an opera singer.
BELOW: Susan tries to complete her jigsaw puzzle in one of the vast echoing rooms of Xanadu. The isolation of Kane and Susan from each other is perfectly expressed.

RASHOMON

JAPAN 1950
DIRECTED BY
AKIRA KUROSAWA

Producer: *Jingo Minoru*
Screenplay: *Shino Hashimoto,*
Akira Kurosawa.
Based on stories by
Ryunosuke Akutagawa
Music: *Fumio Hayasaka*
Photography: *Kazuo Miyagawa*
Daiei. 83 mins

Leading players:
Toshiro Mifune, Machiko Kyo,
Masayuki Mori, Takashi Shimura.

'Beware of staring too long into the abyss,' said the philosopher Nietzsche, 'lest the abyss stare back into you.' This is one of the issues at the heart of Akira Kurosawa's *Rashomon*. A nobleman has been killed in a forest; his wife has been raped; a bandit is accused; a woodcutter seems inadvertently to have witnessed the incident. In flashback these four conflicting accounts of the events seem determined to conceal rather than reveal the truth. Yet the crime seems appalling enough. How can the truth be worse? What is it that each character seems to be hiding?

Rashomon won the top prize at the 1951 Venice Film Festival and subsequently a Hollywood Oscar for best foreign film. For most western observers, it served as a

remarkable introduction to the Japanese cinema. It has enough exoticism to make it seem different and strange: the period setting; the scene whereby the dead nobleman is able to give his testimony through the intermediary of a psychic medium. But it is not so eccentric as to make it inaccessible. Its sophisticated conception of the subjectivity of truth and its use of multiple perspectives on a single incident are reminiscent of *Citizen Kane*.

Rashomon was also a revelation of technical mastery in the Japanese cinema. The story is told in a vividly exciting way, with hectic tracking shots through the forest, sunlight glinting through trees as uncertainly as truth itself from this murky affair, and a relentless Bolero-like score building a palpable air of menace. The performances undoubtedly intensify the tension. Toshiro Mifune's characterization of the bandit conveys a snarling sense of physical threat, like a lion pacing his cage. Masayuki Mori instils the character of the nobleman-warrrior with chilling dignity, and Machiko Kyo's remarkable performance as the wife, with hints of sensuality beneath the decorous façade, contains all the rich ambiguity of the film's main themes. Takashi Shimura, one of Kurosawa's honoured group of players, is the woodcutter.

In a distinguished career, Kurosawa has gone on to elaborate many of the traits that one notices in *Rashomon*: the fascination with extremes of ego and suffering ('I like extremes,' he has said, 'because I find them most fully alive.'); an interest in those personalities who show unshakeable obstinacy in the teeth of adversity; and an unexpected humour and eye for the absurd. In the last part of *Rashomon*, one is made aware of the proximity of tragedy to farce, and given a hint that each character's self-justifying story might be conferring a nobility on behaviour and event that, in reality, turned out to be squalid, silly and demeaning. The film's opening and closing, which frame the action, seem slow and sentimental, but the obsessive return to the forest is both harrowing and hypnotic. The repeated accounts of what happened do not seem repetitious, because the search is not ultimately for the solution of a crime but the key to each individual character. Kurosawa's achievement is to make his analysis of the complex deviousness of human psychology seem as hair-raisingly exciting as a conventional thriller.

RIGHT: A Hollywood writer is fished out of a star's swimming pool. 'He'd always wanted a pool,' says a voice from beyond the grave. 'Well, in the end he got himself a pool, only the price turned out a little high.'

BELOW: Norma Desmond's butler, Max (Erich von Stroheim) ceremonially completes the bizarre burial of Norma's pet chimp.

BOTTOM: Tango on a tiled floor. A lonely dance on New Year's Eve shared by Norma (Gloria Swanson) and Joe (William Holden).

CENTRE: Joe and Norma watch one of her old silent movies on the private screen in her living room. 'And no dialogue,' she purrs. 'We didn't need dialogue – we had faces.'

FAR RIGHT: 'No one ever leaves a star. That's what makes one a star.' When Joe starts to walk out on Norma, she follows him, gun in hand.

BOTTOM RIGHT: 'The dream she had clung to so desperately had enfolded her.' Watched by police and photographers, and to the sound of clicking cameras, Norma, as Salome, descends the staircase.

SUNSET BOULEVARD

USA 1950
DIRECTED BY BILLY WILDER

Producer: *Charles Brackett*
Screenplay: *Charles Brackett,*
Billy Wilder, D. M. Marshman Jr
Music: *Franz Waxman*
Photography: *John F. Seitz*
Paramount. 111 mins

Leading players:
Gloria Swanson, William Holden,
Erich von Stroheim, Nancy Olson,
Cecil B. de Mille.

Through the analysis of a finally destructive relationship between an older woman who is well-to-do and a younger man who is not doing too well, *Sunset Boulevard* presents a contrast between Old and New Hollywood that oscillates between satire and savagery, nostalgia and horror. The older woman is Norma Desmond (Gloria Swanson), a former star of silent cinema whose career receded in the era of talkies and who is now planning a return in a

vehicle of her own devising, *Salome*. The younger man is Joe Gillis (William Holden), a struggling screenwriter who, in return for certain material (and later, sexual) favours, agrees to 'ghost' her screenplay for her in the certainty that it will never be produced.

When Gillis has recognized the star for the first time and commented that 'You used to be big,' Miss Desmond has drawn herself up to deliver one of the most witheringly memorable lines in movie history: 'I *am* big. It's the pictures that got small.' There is a grandeur about Norma Desmond, but the grand gestures are anachronistic in the modern cinema of realism. Her grand mansion is decaying and disintegrating through neglect, rather like the lady herself who has been deserted by a public that once idolized her. In addition to its superlative performances, wonderful wit and ingenious plotting, the achievement of the film is to reveal the tragedy behind the star's façade without sentimentalizing her egomania. Because we are introduced to her through the screenwriter's eyes, we tend gradually to share his complex reactions to her: amused, saddened, exasperated, awed.

Sunset Boulevard is a film about movie history. The casting has all kinds of resonances: Gloria Swanson as Norma, herself a great star of the silent screen, for whom *Sunset Boulevard* is happily a triumphant comeback; Erich von Stroheim as Norma's butler, Max, playing with enormous dignity a man who, like himself, was a great director now forced into a more ignominious role; Cecil B. DeMille as himself, a tough survivor from the silent era, who will greet Norma with genuine warmth on a film set, but no amount of sentiment or friendly feeling would persuade him to touch her 'awful script'. As a portrait of Hollywood, *Sunset Boulevard* touches on some uncomfortable nerves ('We should horsewhip this Wilder,' cried Louis B. Mayer apparently, 'he has brought disgrace on the town that is feeding him!'). It shows a hard, competitive and ruthless community. The writer's claustrophobia intensifies as he tries to escape from a Hollywood that is destroying him. Norma's increasing derangement, as her fear of final rejection creeps nearer to the surface, drives her ever more into a world of illusion. Everything is set for a staggering grand finale. Norma slips over the edge into madness, becomes the Salome of her dreams and transforms her whole world into a sound-stage, whilst the ghost writer (*literally* a ghost now) breathes a beautiful, merciful valediction for her from beyond the grave. Truly, as Norma herself might say, they don't make pictures like this any more.

INDIA
DIRECTED BY SATYAJIT RAY

PATHER PANCHALI (1955)
Screenplay: *Satyajit Ray*
From the novel by
Bidhutibhustan Bandapadhaya
Music: *Ravi Shankar*
Photography: *Subrata Mitra*
APARAJITO (*The Unvanquished*)
(1956) Credits as above
APU SANSAR (*The World of Apu*)
(1959) Credits as above
123 mins; 108 mins; 106 mins

Leading players:
*Kanu, Karuna and Subir Bannerjee,
Soumitra Chatterjee, Sharmila Tagore,
Uma Das Gupta, Chunibala,
Pinaki Sen Gupta, Sumiran Ghosjal,
Shapan Mukerjee.*

If *Rashomon* put Japanese cinema on the map, international recognition of the Indian cinema came with the showing of *Pather Panchali* at the 1956 Cannes Festival. Remarkably, the film had been made on primitive equipment over a period of about four years by people with little or no technical experience. François Truffaut dismissed it as 'Europeanized and insipid', and a London critic ingloriously described it as 'pad, pad, pad through the paddy fields'. But these views were unrepresentative. The film was to prove the first part of perhaps the most celebrated trilogy in film history, *The Apu Trilogy*, which traces the life of the central character Apu from infancy in a poor Bengali village to manhood in the city of Calcutta. With the writer Rabindranath Tagore, who was a close friend of Ray's grandfather, Satyajit Ray can lay claim to being the most acclaimed artist his country has produced this century.

Whilst acknowledging his own cultural origins, Ray's films invariably transcend national boundaries. This is partly because of the thorough grounding in the tradition of European film before his own screen debut. Italian neo-realism was a substantial influence: *Bicycle Thieves*, particularly, 'just gored me', Ray said. The

major inspiration was Jean Renoir, whom Ray met in Calcutta when Renoir was filming *The River*. 'It sounds wonderful, make it, I think it will make a fine film,' he told him when Ray outlined his plans for *Pather Panchali*. There are perceptible affinities between the works and outlooks of both men, in their sensitivity to nature, their unobtrusive camera styles, their generous view of humanity.

People in Ray's films tend to be thoughtless rather than evil, but the effects are devastating. The grandmother dies largely from neglect in *Pather Panchali*, and the mother's illness in *Aparajito* is unnoticed until too late by Apu, who is absorbed with himself and his studies. In *The World of Apu*, the hero writes a novel and marries. But his beloved wife dies in childbirth; the moment when Apu, told of his wife's death, responds by smacking the messenger across the face, is one of the most emotionally violent in all of Ray's work. Tossing the pages of his novel to the wind, Apu sinks into near-suicidal despair, until a reunion with his son recalls his own childhood and enforces recognition that the cycle of life must go on.

Ravi Shankar's music, the fresh-eyed photography of field and sky, the unifying visual motifs of river and railway, contribute to a trilogy whose observation has incredible purity. Citing a piece Tagore had written for him when he was seven, Ray has said he has always sought the 'dewdrop in a blade of grass', the presence of the essential thing in a very small detail. What was once said about Tagore – 'He has spoken out of life itself, and that is why we give him our love' – can also be applied to Satyajit Ray.

OPPOSITE, TOP: Apu's father (Kanu Banerjee) in a dramatic moment from *Pather Panchali*.
CENTRE: A scene between Apu's mother (Karuna Banerjee) and Apu's sister, Durga (Uma Das Gupta).
BOTTOM: The withered old woman (Chunibali) during a gentler moment with Apu's mother. Later she will be allowed to die from neglect, as she becomes an increasing burden on the family.
TOP LEFT: A pensive moment for Apu (played at this stage of the film by Pinaki Sen Gupta), who watches his father at the religious rites by the river in the holy city of Benares. From *Aparajito*.
RIGHT: Apu (Smaran Ghosal) reads a book on Livingstone. He is proving to be a successful scholar but his mother's illness summons him back to the village. From *Aparajito*.
ABOVE: Apu (Soumitra Chatterjee) with his bride (Sharmila Tagore). From the third part of the trilogy, *The World of Apu*.
RIGHT: In a mood of suicidal despair after the death of his wife, Apu moves through a forest glade and, standing on a hill top, tosses the pages of his manuscript to the wind.

L'AVVENTURA

ITALY 1960

DIRECTED BY
MICHELANGELO ANTONIONI

Producer: *Cino Del Duca*
Screenplay:
*Michelangelo Antonioni,
Elio Bartolini, Tonino Guerra*
Music: *Giovanni Fusco*
Photography: *Aldo Scavarda*
145 mins

Leading players:
*Monica Vitti, Gabriele Ferzetti,
Lea Massari.*

Michelangelo Antonioni is that rare thing: an intellectual with a camera. His films are about the disjunction between material comfort and emotional emptiness. Most of his characters are wealthy, successful, intelligent, who nevertheless feel a gathering dissatisfaction with their lives. How do you find fulfilment? How best can you adapt to the society in which you live? More than any other film-maker of the early 60s, Antonioni made alienation fashionable. He also gave it a striking visual form, the positioning of the camera making each shot an eloquent comment on the tension between protagonist and environment.

L'Avventura concerns the disappearance of a young woman, Anna (Lea Massari), and the guilty love that develops between Anna's friend, Claudia (Monica Vitti) and Anna's lover, Sandro (Gabriele Ferzetti) in their unavailing search for her. She never reappears: Antonioni has described the film as a detective story told back to front. (When asked what happened to her, he replied: 'I don't know. Someone told me she committed suicide but I don't believe it.') Anna's disappearance infects the subsequent relationships and initiates a whole cycle of sexual betrayal, in which Claudia feels guilty about her affair with Sandro, and Sandro (professionally frustrated in his job as an architect's surveyor)

is unfaithful to Claudia. In the famous final scene, they come together in what Antonioni called 'a feeling of shared pity', Claudia framed against a background of a dormant volcano in the distance, Sandro staring at a blank wall.

Antonioni has often been compared with a favourite novelist of his, Scott Fitzgerald. Both are acute analysts of the spiritual malaise of the rich, and of heroes who are failed artists. Both create worlds of brittle surfaces that echo with the sound of loveless money. Like Fitzgerald, Antonioni is remarkably good at making links between the moral behaviour of the characters and the society in which they move, and between the sexual life of the individual and his or her private personality.

At the time, *L'Avventura* seemed a somewhat steamy study of modern erotic decadence. The impermanent and unstable relationships seemed symptomatic of a world, as Antonioni said, filled more with dead feelings than live ones. The tense sexual jealousies of other major films of the decade, like Polanski's *A Knife in the Water* (1961) and Chabrol's *Les Biches* (1969) owed much to Antonioni's example. There is even a trace of *L'Avventura* in a popular film like *Picnic at Hanging Rock* (1975), which is also about an inexplicable disappearance on a rock,

also has a palpable air of languid sensuality, and is also about a search that trails away into suggestiveness and enigma. Nowadays, Antonioni's observations on the anguish of the affluent might look less sympathetic. Nevertheless, one can still admire the imaginative way the film proceeds on mood, nuance and atmosphere rather than plot. The island search sequence, with its cumulative atmosphere of desolation and death, looks as brilliant as ever. And nothing could date the performance of the great Monica Vitti, who is the lamp that gives the film its glow of humanity and emotional warmth.

OPPOSITE, TOP: The last conversation between Anna (Lea Massari) and Sandro (Gabrielle Ferzetti) before Anna mysteriously disappears.
BOTTOM LEFT: Rich and bored passengers from the cruise – Patrizia (Esmeralda Ruspoli, with dog), Raimondo (Lelio Luttazi, centre) and Giulia (Dominique Blanchar, second from right) – join forces to explore the island.
CENTRE: Sandro's architectural ambitions have been reawakened and he goes to the local museum in Noto to seek inspiration, only to find it closed. Note Antonioni's eye here for architecture, setting and the odd visual detail, used to express a mood.
TOP RIGHT: Corrado (James Addams) and Sandro discuss with the police how best to search for Anna.
BOTTOM RIGHT: Claudia (Monica Vitti) on the train home. The search for Anna has ended in failure. Soon she will take Anna's place as Sandro's lover. 'No other actress inspires me like Monica,' said Antonioni of his leading actress. 'Without her, I don't know how I could have made *L'Avventura* – nobody else would have been right.'

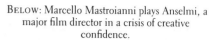

BELOW: Marcello Mastroianni plays Anselmi, a major film director in a crisis of creative confidence.
TOP LEFT: Two of the many women in Anselmi's life, the ageing chanteuse, Jacqueline (Yvonne Casadei) and Rosella (Rosella Falk), who both appear in Anselmi's fantasy harem.
BOTTOM LEFT: An encounter with the Cardinal (Tito Massini), who is visiting the spa where Anselmi is staying. When he kisses the Cardinal's ring, it triggers a flashback to his encounter as a boy with the prostitute La Saraghina.
BOTTOM RIGHT: A circus band plays against the background of the spaceship scaffolding, a set for the movie that Anselmi fails to make. At the end of the film characters from his past will descend from the tower and parade in front of Anselmi.
OPPOSITE: A memory from Anselmi's childhood, as his mind recalls his fascination with La Saraghina (Edra Gale).

8½

ITALY 1963
DIRECTED BY
FEDERICO FELLINI

Producer: *Angelo Rizzoli*
Screenplay: *Federico Fellini,
Ennio Flaiano, Tullio Pinelli,
Brunello Rondi*
Music: *Nino Rota*
Photography: *Gianni Di Venanzo*
135 mins

Leading players:
*Marcello Mastroianni,
Anouk Aimee, Claudia Cardinale,
Rosella Falk.*

What should a film-maker do if suffering from a creative block? Federico Fellini knows: he should make a film about a director suffering from a creative block. The hero of *8½* is a director, Anselmi (Marcello Mastroianni) who is stuck for ideas on his new film. The title suggests that Fellini intends *8½* as a self-portrait (this was the number of films he had made to date). But the crucial difference is that, whereas Anselmi decides eventually not to make his film, Fellini has completed his, triumphantly.

8½ is a portrait of the artist as a middle-aged man. It assumes – and demonstrates – that a film director is not a hired hand but an artist deserving the same attention and esteem of a writer or painter. It is also a portrait of the film director as superstar. After the notorious success of Fellini's previous film, *La Dolce Vita* (1960), *8½* takes for granted that an audience will be fascinated by the creative agonies of its director.

Anselmi is not only a portrait of Fellini. He is any talented artist with a creative crisis, trying not to lie in his art, faced with the infinite problems of selection, and ransacking his own life and acquaintances for ideas and inspiration. At a press conference, Anselmi is driven by the aggressive questioning into imagining his own suicide. 'I really have nothing to say, but I'm going to say it anyway,' he cries, torn between defiance at critical sniping yet fear of artistic impotence.

Anselmi also represents not only the artist but any man at a crisis in middle-age. Anselmi's fear of flickering creativity is clearly linked to his awareness of declining sexual potency and of his own mortality. His memories are mixed up with images of the women in his life, past and present. Desperately he tries to summon these visions into an order that will give his life meaning, avoid the mistakes of immaturity, rejuvenate him personally and creatively.

Like *Citizen Kane*, *8½* is a quest for identity which leaps audaciously in time. It also lurches between fantasy and reality. A nightmare about being stuck in his car correlates to Anselmi's feeling of artistic constriction. A fantasy role of lion-tamer is a metaphor for his wish to control the women in his life and to whip the conflicting images in his head obediently into some sort of artistic shape. It is also an image of Fellini as supreme ringmaster, characteristically comparing circus and cinema, with their bizarre people and their similar mixture of spectacle, risk and reality.

It might seem a forbidding film, but Fellini has always operated instinctively rather than intellectually and encouraged people to feel his films emotionally rather than dissect them analytically. 'If you are moved by it,' he says, 'you don't need to have it explained to you. If not, no explanation can make you moved by it.' The enduring fascination of *8½* testifies to Fellini's skill in bringing to life his visual imagination and universalizing his private world.

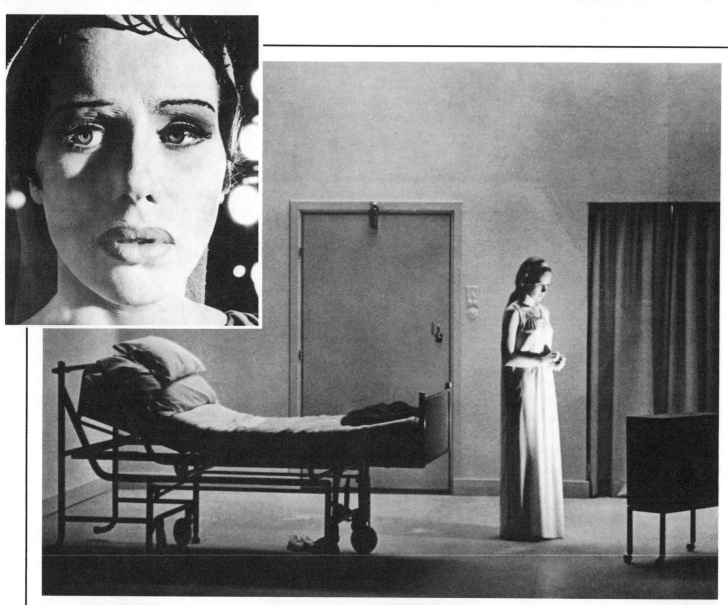

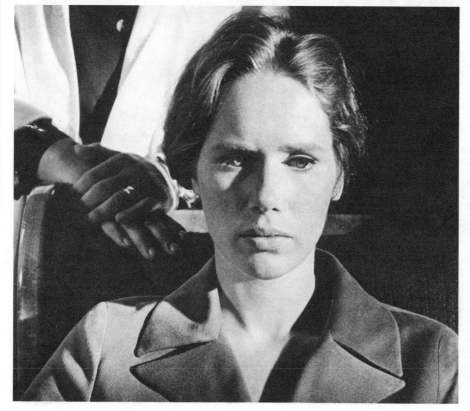

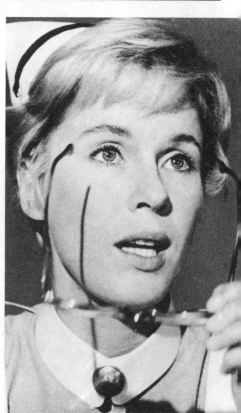

PERSONA

SWEDEN 1966
DIRECTED BY
INGMAR BERGMAN

Screenplay: *Ingmar Bergman*
Music: *Lars Johan Werle*
Photography: *Sven Nykvist*
84 mins

Leading players:
*Bibi Andersson, Liv Ullmann,
Gunnar Björnstrand.*

Ingmar Bergman has described *Persona* as 'a creation that saved its creator'. At a period when he felt ill and dispirited, he began sifting through assorted dreams and memories. They gradually formed into a fable about someone who could not go on being an artist. An actress (Liv Ullmann) breaks down on stage and refuses to talk to anyone: a nurse (Bibi Andersson) is assigned to look after her. As this idea developed and the creative current flowed, Bergman realized he had the strength to continue.

On one level, *Persona* is a remarkable character study of two people having difficulty in confronting their own insecurities and fears. The actress's withdrawal from them is signified by her silence. The nurse slowly becomes undermined by that silence, which seems to represent a void of non-communication that begins to threaten her own identity. The silence seems to force painful confessions out of her (a story of an orgy on the beach recalled in what Bergman calls 'a tone of shameful lust'). It arouses an unsuspected pent-up violence. The actress appears to the nurse partly as tender lover, partly as blood-sucking vampire, peeling away the mask of her personality, forcing an awareness of the infinite layers of confusion and terror in the human mind.

On a more philosophical, artistic level, *Persona* is a study of role-playing, in which the actress decides to become the silent audience and the nurse is suddenly the performer, revealing her secret self through the persistent monologue demanded of her. One might say that the nurse represents 'Life', which the artist coldly and selfishly watches and scavenges for material. Certainly the role of art and the artist is central to *Persona*. Bergman often reminds us that we are watching a film, and indeed parallels our situation with that of the actress at one stage, where she watches in horror a TV image of a monk's self-immolation in Saigon. Are we all impotent watchers of the horror of the world? In examining such painful events, is the artist performing a relevant function or is he simply indulging his own sensitivity? *Persona* is an interrogation of the usefulness of the artist in a complex, cruel modern civilization.

Bergman's art is a sort of clinic of the soul. His characters are patients who undergo a terrifying yet hopefully therapeutic experience. Creation of this order, where the darkest areas of human motivation are rooted out in order to understand them and to come to terms with them, is an obviously painful process. Yet there is an exhilaration about an artist like Bergman who can endure such fire and still continue to create. He has always been an incomparable director of actresses (the performances of Bibi Andersson and Liv Ullmann in *Persona* are beyond praise), an increasingly fine technician, and a cinéaste who has devised new forms in which to convey complex psychology. 'My kingdom is a small one,' he says to those who find his themes limited and repetitive, 'but I am King there.'

OPPOSITE, TOP LEFT: Liv Ullmann as the actress Elisabeth Vogler in the role of Electra. After this performance she retreats into total silence.
TOP RIGHT: Elisabeth Vogler watches television in her room. At the sight of the self-immolation of a Buddhist monk on the screen, she will scream loudly and piercingly.
BOTTOM RIGHT: Elisabeth Vogler sits in the chair whilst, behind her, her doctor diagnoses her condition. 'You can cut yourself off,' says the doctor. 'Then you don't have to play a part . . . or so you think.'
BOTTOM RIGHT: Bibi Andersson as Sister Alma, the nurse assigned to care for Mrs Vogler. 'I think art is tremendously important in life,' she says hesitantly to Elisabeth, 'particularly for people who are in some kind of difficulty.'
BELOW LEFT: Alma and Elisabeth on the terrace. The apprehension in Elisabeth's eyes and the dark clothing indicate that their relationship is deteriorating.
BELOW: Ingmar Bergman directing one of his players.

ACKNOWLEDGEMENTS

The Publishers would like to thank Michelle Snapes and the staff at The National Film Archive for their invaluable assistance during the compilation of this book.

All the black and white and colour photographs featured in this book have been provided by THE NATIONAL FILM ARCHIVE, London with the exception of the following sources:

Black and white photographs
The Hamlyn Group Picture Library: 109, 112, 113, 154 top right; *The Kobal Collection, London*: endpapers, 9 bottom, 17 bottom, 36–37, 72–73, 79 top, 94 bottom, 95 top, 100 bottom, 101 bottom, 105 bottom left, 148 top, 157, 160 bottom left, 161 top, 168, 175. *David Shipman*: 10, 12 bottom, 35 top left, 48 top, 51 bottom left, 52,56, 64 top right, 87 bottom left, 88 top, 89 bottom, 93 top right, 93 bottom left, 95 bottom right, 96 top, 107 centre, 136 bottom, 144, 146 top, 155 top, 172 top right, 173 top, 181 top right, 181 center.

Colour photographs
The Hamlyn Group Picture Library: 82–83, 98, 167 bottom left, 167 top & inset, 166; *The Kobal Collection, London*: 42 bottom, 81 top left, 127 top, 167 bottom right; *David Shipman*: 49 top & bottom, 51 bottom right, 56 top left; All photographs on pages 62–63 by kind permission of *Walt Disney Productions*.

Any unintentional acknowledgement omission is hereby apologised for in advance, and we should of course be pleased to correct any errors in acknowledgements in any future edition of this book.

Front Jacket: The Kobal Collection, London.
Back Jacket: The National Film Archive, London.